WA

G000115862

Also by Rob Warner

21st Century Church
Alive in the Spirit
Prepare for Revival
Together We Stand (with Clive Calver)

Walking with God

Discovering a deeper spirituality in prayer

Rob Warner

Hodder & Stoughton
LONDON SYDNEY AUCKLAND

Unless otherwise indicated, Scripture quotations are taken from the HOLY
BIBLE, NEW INTERNATIONAL VERSION. Copyright © 1973, 1978, 1984 by
International Bible Society. Used by permission. All rights reserved.

Copyright © Rob Warner 1998

First published in Great Britain 1998

The right of Rob Warner to be identified as the
Author of the Work has been asserted by him in
accordance with the Copyright, Designs and
Patents Act 1988.

10 9 8 7 6 5 4 3 2 1

All rights reserved. No part of this publication may be
reproduced, stored in a retrieval system, or transmitted,
in any form or by any means without the prior written
permission of the publisher, nor be otherwise circulated in
any form of binding or cover other than that in which it
is published and without a similar condition being imposed
on the subsequent purchaser.

British Library Cataloguing in Publication Data
A record for this book is available from the British Library

ISBN 0 340 71015 2

Typeset by Hewer Text Composition Services, Edinburgh
Printed and bound in Great Britain by
Clays Ltd, St Ives plc, Bungay, Suffolk

Hodder and Stoughton Ltd
A Division of Hodder Headline PLC
338 Euston Road
London NW1 3BH

This book is dedicated to Ernest and Joyce,
my dear parents,
who first taught me the Lord's Prayer as a young child
and encouraged me to pray each night.

Contents

O for a closer walk with God,
A calm and heavenly frame,
A light to shine upon the road
That leads me to the Lamb!

Where is the blessedness I knew
When first I saw the Lord?
Where is the soul-refreshing view
Of Jesus and his Word?

What peaceful hours I once enjoyed!
How sweet their memory still!
But they have left an aching void
The world can never fill.

The dearest idol I have known,
Whate'er that idol be,
Help me to tear it from thy throne,
And worship only thee.

So shall my walk be close with God,
Calm and serene my frame:
So purer light shall mark the road
That leads me to the Lamb.

William Cowper, 1731–1800

Introduction

This is not a book for prayer specialists, who spend every waking moment in effortless prayer and find nothing in life easier than communion with God. It has been written for ordinary people with busy lives who long for a deeper sense of spiritual reality and vitality, but who battle to find time to pray and ways to keep prayer fresh and alive. Nor has it been written by a prayer specialist. I often find prayer a struggle, and the little progress I have made in prayer has been very slow. If you want to read the writings of a sublime mystic, you must turn elsewhere. If you want to read of a very ordinary Christian's discoveries in prayer, then I pray that this little book may enrich your experience of prayer.

Francis de Sales surely summed up in the preface to his *Introduction to the Devout Life* the experience of nearly every writer on prayer, acknowledging both his personal limitations and his holy ambition: 'I write about the devout life without being devout myself, though I certainly desire to be so, and it is my desire for devotion that encourages me to write ... I hope that while I am leading God's beloved sheep to the waters of devotion, he in his goodness will make my soul his own.'

It is one thing to believe in Christ, another to seek to live close to him. Whatever Jesus' many other remarkable qualities, he was unmistakably a man of prayer and therefore, in his humanity, a man of God. In an age when many are flocking to stress clinics and relaxation courses, we need to rediscover the inestimable richness of the art and discipline of Christian prayer. Prayer creates the still centre of being, the fertile ground upon which we can cultivate effective and creative living.

I have written this book with the intention that it will prove useful in a variety of settings. Some will want to read it straight through, like any other book. Some may find it useful as a course book for a series of home group studies, perhaps through Lent. Others may choose to read each chapter as a series of daily readings. To assist such an approach, each chapter is split into six short sections, followed by a Bible meditation.

At the end of each chapter I have included one or two fine prayers from the past, together with some great devotional poetry and classical hymns. The poetry, mainly from the seventeenth century, is well known to me from my days of studying literature, but is probably little known by most Christians. The hymns are included because they too are becoming a neglected resource for prayer. It is a cultural inevitability that many churches will no longer use many classical hymns in public worship: younger generations increasingly find the words difficult and the old tunes interminable. However, it would be a terrible squandering of a great historical treasure chest of devotion if these hymns disappeared altogether from Christian consciousness. They are an invaluable part of our heritage in prayer.

Great devotional poetry has the ability to do two things: to express my own present circumstances before God with a greater precision, subtlety and richness than I can find in my own words; and to enable me to understand and even experience imaginatively spiritual conditions that I have not yet encountered in my own life. Some readers will enjoy reading reflectively every single poem and hymn found in the collections at the end of each chapter. Others may prefer to select one that seems particularly appropriate for personal meditation, coming back to explore the others at a later time.

In addition to a hymn selected to complement the theme of each chapter, I have also selected a hymn for every chapter from two of the greatest English hymn writers, Wesley and Cowper. Charles Wesley (1707–88) succeeded triumphantly in combining an astonishingly prolific output with a remarkable, sustained freshness. A vibrantly positive spirit and an encyclopedic grasp of Scripture characterise his wonderful poetry, which has had the power to inspire many believers to prayer and praise in every succeeding generation. New hymns from Wesley's pen regularly fuelled the revival fires of the Great Awakening, and those who long for revival at the dawn of the third millennium can discover much of its distinctive spiritual ardour in reading his poetry.

William Cowper (1731–1800) is a much more brooding poet, and yet, in a life often clouded with depression, Cowper managed to retain and express a sense of hope through sadness, of divine grace in the face of human weakness. We live in an era when everyone from advertisers to politicians and preachers can subscribe to the need to be remorselessly upbeat, positive and cheerful. For everyone who sometimes finds life difficult and marked by an uphill struggle, there is an antiseptic bite, a cleansing, sharp-eyed realism found in Cowper's devotional poetry, giving voice to a faith that is melancholy, yet resilient.

This book would not have been possible without an annual opportunity for several years to lecture on prayer at the London Institute for Contemporary Christianity. I am indebted to Ernest Lucas and Simon Steer for extending the kind invitation to me to contribute in this small way to their programme. I am also enormously grateful for the privilege of working with the wonderful international body of students at the Institute, whose many insights and explorations of prayer have enriched me greatly.

Walking with God makes no claim to be an exhaustive manual of prayer. In particular, I made the deliberate choice not to explore at any length in this book either the Lord's Prayer or the Lord's Supper because, to do them justice, these two great themes deserve many chapters of their own. If *Walking with God* meets with sufficient popularity I hope to explore them in a subsequent book.

My prayer is simply that as you read this book it will prove to be more than a theoretical exercise. I hope that these chapters will inspire you to explore further the many avenues of prayer, perhaps including some paths that are less familiar within the cultural style of your local church, as you seek in daily living to pursue a closer walk with God.

Rob Warner
July 1997

CHAPTER I

KNOWING GOD AS FATHER

Growing in relationship

Heal us, Immanuel; hear our prayer;
We wait to feel thy touch:
Deep-wounded souls to thee repair,
And, Saviour, we are such.

Our faith is feeble, we confess;
We faintly trust thy word:
But wilt thou pity us the less?
Be that far from thee, Lord!

Remembering him who once applied
With trembling for relief;
'Lord, I believe!' with tears he cried,
'O help my unbelief!'

She, too, who touched thee in the press,
And healing virtue stole,
Was answered: 'Daughter, go in peace,
Thy faith has made thee whole.'

Like her, with hopes and fears we come
To touch thee, if we may:
O send us not despairing home,
Send none unhealed away.

William Cowper

1

The Problem with Fathers

In movies and soaps, novels and documentaries, problem fathers abound in the late twentieth century. Past generations were accustomed to the common tragedy of children losing their fathers to premature death, and the reduced number of such casualties today does nothing to diminish the trauma for those children who suffer the loss of a parent who dies young. In the late twentieth century, an increasing number of fathers across the Western world have become absent through divorce. Some decline to assume any parental responsibility from the moment the pregnancy is first discovered or announced, and so remain ever unknown by the children to whose conception they contributed. Others reject their children later, turning their backs upon a difficult relationship, whether with the children themselves or with their mother. Worse still, many more than once we feared or imagined have been discovered to have been abused by their own father, whether sexually or physically.

Conditional love sends a blight upon other children that can leave them wounded even in adult years, with the unmistakable message that a father's love must be earned through climbing a mountain of accomplishments, whether sporting or academic, in the arts or in business. The trouble with conditional love is that the goalposts seem continually to be on the move: there is always another mountain to climb before love can ever be won securely. Other fathers are habitually critical, always rebuking, always pointing out the faults and failings of their offspring. The traditional warning of British mothers served to reinforce this tendency to automatic negativity – 'Wait till your father gets home!'

The final major category of dysfunctional fathers is the remote. Some are so far out of touch with their own emotions that they have little idea how to express love and affection to their children. Some have never learned how to relate to children. Some are so busy providing for their children at work that they have neglected to spend time with them. Children's bedrooms across the Western world are littered with the latest consumer goodies, but many children suffer an emptiness of heart that electronic gadgetry can never satisfy, for they are growing up knowing little or nothing of a father's love.

Faced with such a catalogue of failed and problem fathers, is it naive, foolish or even cruel for Christians to speak of God as 'Father'? Is it no more than an excess of patriarchal religion? Or does it represent extreme pastoral insensitivity, a blatant disregard for the victims of the follies and failures of modern fatherhood?

Freud recognised that many people's concept of God is revealing, as a projection of their relationship with their own father. Like a picture on an acetate thrown up on to a large screen, what's wrong in the parent–child dynamic can be writ large in our instinctive understanding of what God is like. For Christians this is a critical issue. We believe in a real God, not just a projected neurosis. But inasmuch as Freud's analysis is correct, there is a very real danger that a damaged relationship with an earthly father will intrude upon our spirituality, grievously distorting our concept of divinity. The deep wounds of inadequate parenting can ensnare, scar, or even cripple our capacity for relationship with God.

The logic of projection cuts two ways. Just as those with failed fathers may struggle to relate to God as Father, there may be a hidden snare for those whose fathers have been exemplary. Bill told me of his wonderful relationship with his dad, who had died a couple of years before. 'Whenever I pray to God the Father,' Bill explained, 'I think of my dear old dad.' Maybe Bill's fond memories were beneficial, enriching his understanding of the fatherliness of God. Yet I was unsure. There was at least a slight possibility of some kind of unconscious idolatry, in which an ostensible prayer to the Christian God slipped imperceptibly into a form of oblique ancestor worship, in adoration of his devoted, departed dad. Whenever we constrict the mystery and majesty of the living God within the narrow confines of our own parental projections, good or bad, in narrowing our concept of God we constrain not merely our understanding but also our potential for spiritual development and enrichment.

Practical meditation

Could my image of God the Father be distorted or constrained in any way by my childhood experiences?

2

Abba and Baby Talk

Before babies learn to speak, their communication skills are already developing fast. Burbles and smiles, grimaces, shrieks and tantrums all play their part in eloquently conveying the need for a changed nappy, the removal of some thoroughly repulsive food, or a hasty return to Mum's arms from the unwelcome attention of a stranger. When you are not feeling too hassled by the imperious urgency of a baby's latest whim, their skilful pre-verbal communication is astounding and often very amusing.

Alongside such active communication babies begin to play with their voices, forming random patterns of hard and soft sounds. At this stage fathers tend to become suddenly attentive, waiting for the moment when the baby calls them by name. The baby has known the mother's voice and heartbeat from within the womb, her smell and touch from the first feed, and so there is a much more immediate intimacy with Mum than with Dad in the early weeks and months of life. It is therefore extremely unlikely that a baby will consciously seek to speak to Dad first. But try telling that to the attentive male, doting on the first recognisable word formed on the lips of his offspring!

Many languages have a number of names by which to address a male parent. In English, they include Dad, Daddy, Father,

Papa, Pa, Pater, Old Man and even Sir. The simplest repetitive combination of a consonant and vowel is what we normally expect to hear from the lips of a baby: Dada in English, Papa in French. For the Jews, not only in the Aramaic dialect of Jesus' time but also in modern Hebrew, the equivalent infant term for a father is Abba. I remember vividly in Tel Aviv airport seeing the enthusiastic rush of two young children towards their father whose plane had recently landed. 'Abba, abba!' was the cry on their lips as they embraced their father and welcomed him home.

When Jesus spoke of knowing God as Father, he spoke in terms no Jew had dared to use before. God was the Almighty, the Lord of hosts, the Sovereign One, awesome in his majesty and might. Some rabbis had dared to make a bold comparison, suggesting that in some ways God could be said to be 'like an Abba'. But Jesus described God directly and simply as 'Abba'. It was a way of referring to God that was unique to Jesus, an astonishing new dimension to Jewish spirituality.

We have lost the shock of the new. When Jesus spoke of God as 'Abba' it was radical. When Christians today speak of God as 'Almighty *Father*' we tend to formalise the title. A Christian workman was fixing our windows and complained to me about the informality with which some Christians address God. 'I know Jesus spoke of God as "Abba",' he protested, 'but surely that means something like "Dear Lord"!' In our desire to preserve a rightful reverence before the awesome majesty and holiness of the divine presence, we have tended to neglect or even abandon the astonishing intimacy that Jesus taught. When Jesus reveals God as Father, he opens up to us possibilities of childlike intimacy, without the slightest encouragement of any indulgence of childishness.

'Abba' does not have exactly the same connotations as 'Dada' or 'Daddy'. The word used by Jewish infants is habitually used by Jewish adults when addressing their father, to a much greater extent than English-speaking adults address their father as 'Daddy'. This term of affection is therefore not exclusively infantile, but can be used to continue to express that privileged intimacy with a father first discovered in infancy, which can then be enjoyed and sustained in the adult relationship between parent and child.

Jesus never mustered arguments for the existence of God. Instead he invited his followers to discover closeness with the Creator, a loving and trusting relationship with the Lord of hosts. As a young child is secure in the love of his Abba, Jesus lived in father–child closeness with the living God. This was far more than a radical innovation in theology or a unique spirituality, for Jesus offered to initiate his followers into a similar intimacy with the heavenly Father.

Pause for thought

Consider how it feels for a small child to enjoy time with their dad. How might such intimacy inform your walk with your Father in heaven?

3

God's Fatherliness

There is never any suggestion in the Bible that talk of God as Father defines divinity within the categories of human gender. It is together that men and women are made in God's image (Gen. 1:27). Within the Godhead there is therefore found the essence of maleness and femaleness. And yet there is far more to God than this, for divinity transcends the limitations of humanity, including our sexuality. God is neither male as opposed to female, nor female as opposed to male, but is rather *the God beyond male and female*, encompassing yet transcending human personhood.

We speak of God in personal terms, not because God is a person – or rather three persons in one – in exactly the same terms as us, within the specific and limited category of human personhood. What we seek to express is the truth that God is personal and we can know God personally, even though divine personhood transcends the limits of human personality. When we speak of God we are therefore obliged to use personal pronouns – he, him and his – not because we wish to suggest that God is confined within the limits of human gender, but because we could not possibly use impersonal pronouns of the Supreme Being, the source of all love, who is infinitely more personal and more relational than any human being could ever be.

When Jesus prays to God as Abba, dimensions of personhood other than gender are being emphasised. There is a direct simplicity in the opening of the Lord's Prayer. While others may pile up fine-sounding phrases, eloquently extolling the majestic virtues and prowess of the Almighty, Jesus gets straight to the relational point – 'Our Father in heaven' (Matt. 6:9). Not for Jesus the accumulation of honorific titles in a circumlocutory or tautological preamble. Instead he takes us directly into a close and open relationship, expressing intimacy with the God who reveals himself as Father.

Relating to a good father is rooted in security and trust. Because I know that my father can be trusted to give me good things, I will not shrink into the shadows if he enters a room carrying a present with my name upon it. Jesus used this familiar experience in his parable of parental reliability. The trustworthy human father will not give his children bad presents when asked for good things. A request for an egg or a fish will not lead to being given a stone or a scorpion. Jesus then delivers his punch-line: 'If you, then, though you are evil, know how to give good gifts to your children, how much more will your Father in heaven give good gifts to those who ask him!' (Matt. 7:9–11). Luke records a variant on the saying, in which Jesus emphasised that the Holy Spirit is nothing less than the best gift that could possibly be given to the children of the heavenly Father (Luke 11:11–13).

Jesus does everything he possibly can to convey this simple message: Abba can be trusted. We don't need to pay lip service to divine fatherliness while keeping cautious watch for divine thunderbolts. The ancient Egyptian epic tale of the flood spoke of impulsive, short-tempered gods who became irritated by the noise of humankind and decided to send a flood in order to have a quiet life in heaven. Homer, Virgil and Ovid wrote of Greek and Roman gods who were capricious, lecherous, jealous and even treacherous in their dealings with men and women. But Jesus speaks of an altogether different kind of deity. Abba Father invites us to enter into a secure and trusting intimacy, in which we can be confident that his dealings with us will never be casual or callous, forgetful or malevolent. As the Jewish children at Tel Aviv airport ran to the arms of their father and gladly received the gifts that celebrated his return, we can run to the arms of our Father in heaven and gladly receive the gifts of love that are offered through the Holy Spirit.

Pause for thought

How can we grow in confidence in the love of Abba, our Father?

4

Jesus and the Father

Jesus spoke often of his own relationship with the Father. He explained that he did only what the Father set before him (John 6:38). Despite the immense quantity and urgency of needs that pressed upon Jesus every day from the crowds who made constant demands upon him, it was the call of the Father that gave him his sense of focus. Serenity in the face of many demands is a direct result of intimacy with the Father. Knowing the Father's calling releases us from the tyrannous clamour of conflicting and even impossible expectations that others can place upon our lives.

As well as intimacy, focus and obedience, Jesus claimed an exclusive relationship with the Father. Those who deny him, he will in turn deny before 'my Father in heaven' (Matt. 10:33). The Father has committed all things to the Son. The Father and the Son have a unique mutual understanding and depth of direct relationship, beyond what is possible for any ordinary human being with the living God. Our knowing the Father is dependent upon the initiative of the Son: we can only know the Father if the Son chooses to reveal him to us (Matt. 11:27).

This delicate balancing of continuity and discontinuity between Jesus and his disciples is captured shortly before the ascension when Jesus explained that he was going to 'my Father and your Father' (John 20:17). Because of Jesus' unique relationship with the Father, he can extend to us the possibility of a new kind of closeness with the living God.

We still have the problem of what God the Father is like. Is intimacy with the Father trapped within the concept of fatherliness that we derive from our own experiences of being fathered? Are those with disappointing or even destructive childhood encounters with human fathers condemned to an inability to secure any positive and fulfilling intimacy with their Father in heaven? As Jesus spoke once again of the Father, during his last week in Jerusalem leading up to the cross, some measure of confusion was apparent among Jesus' closest disciples. Philip gave voice to their underlying frustration: 'Lord, show us the Father and that will be enough for us' (John 14:8).

Jesus' reply captures the heart of his unique relationship with the Father. He is not only in constant communion with the Father, praying at all times. He is not only the perfect servant of his Father, obedient at all times. More than that, Jesus claims to be the supreme and direct revelation of the Father, not only in his doctrine, his ethics or his actions, but in his essential being – 'Anyone who has seen me has seen the Father' (John 14:9). In the character of Jesus, the character of the Father is revealed.

In Jesus' baptism, the Father revealed the Son. 'This is my Son whom I love; with him I am well pleased' (Matt. 3:17). In Jesus' life, the Son reveals the Father. Jesus' own claim is quite explicit and unmistakable: if we want to understand the Fatherhood of God, we must begin not by looking at our own experiences of being fathered, whether gloriously good or lamentably deficient. Instead, we must begin with the life of Jesus. To those who have enjoyed good fathers, there is a discipline in defining our concept of God as Father through a single-minded focus on the character of Jesus. To those whose experiences of human fathers have been less than happy, the same disciplined focus upon Jesus as the revelation of the Father can become the means to liberation from the past and to discovering a new hope for the future. Knowing God as Father need not be fatally and permanently flawed for anyone by a tragic history of childhood trauma.

In our ordinary use of the familiar concept of fatherhood we begin with our experience of what a father is like, both personally and culturally. But Jesus' teaching also has intriguing implications for our thinking about the best ways of expressing human fatherhood. While a human father is where our understanding of fatherhood begins to develop, the ultimate source of fatherhood is to be found with God. Therefore, Jesus not only reveals God as Father, he also reveals true fatherhood. If we want to develop a thoroughly Christian understanding of divine fatherhood, we need to begin with Jesus. Equally, if we want to develop a thoroughly Christian understanding of human fatherhood, Jesus must once again become our starting point.

It is not that human fathers reveal God the Father. Rather, God the Father reveals himself in his Son, and that same Son reveals the essential character of truly humane fatherhood. More than that, since men and women are together and equally made in the image of God, in the character of Jesus is found the supreme model for all human parenthood, male and female alike.

In every generation some have indulged in fantasy inventions as substitutes for the real Jesus. There has been the European imperialist Jesus; the American capitalist Jesus; the Che Guevara Jesus; even the footballing genius Jesus in a recent painting of a Manchester United star!

One theologian complained that many of his fellow theologians indulged in similar subjective tendencies. He compared them to men looking into a deep well, each seeing a reflection of his own face in the waters below and then describing what they saw as the true face of Jesus. Christians and non-Christians alike can run the risk of substituting subjective unrealities in place of the real Jesus.

So how do we get as close as possible to the real Jesus who reveals the Father? The answer is clear. We can get no closer to Jesus than the primary documents of the New Testament. Just as the Son reveals the Father, it is the Gospels that supremely reveal the Son. For a fuller understanding of the Fatherhood of God, there is no substitute for prayerful reflection in the light of a careful, thorough and regular reading of the Gospels.

A piano tuner has a necessary and repeated task, bringing a piano back into tune not only with itself but with other instruments. In a similar way, the disciplined study of the Gospels provides the perfect pitch to which we need often to return, redefining and retuning not only our concept of God as Father but also our model of Christian and truly humane parenthood. Jesus Christ is the determinative revelation of the Father.

Pause for thought

List six characteristics typical of fathers in your culture. How do these compare with the character and priorities of Jesus?

5

The Spirit and the Father

While Jesus relates to God as Father by right, as the Son of God incarnate, he makes possible for us a new kind of relationship with God that was not ours by birth. In this new experience, the gift of the Holy Spirit is crucial, for he comes to us as the Spirit of adoption. The legal status of adoption in the Roman Empire was clearly defined. If a child was living in your household, but not as one of your children, their status was wholly inferior. But once their formal adoption was announced there was no going back. From that moment the adopted child had equal rights and equal status with your natural children. The adopted child entered fully into the entitlements of all the children in the family.

The Spirit of adoption is given to believers as an experiential sign and demonstration of our new standing before the Father. The presence of the Spirit is God's own guarantee that a new relationship has been entered into, a new status has been secured. This is not a fleeting encounter, for God the Father binds himself to believers in his Son as surely as a Roman father bound himself to his adopted children.

Paul speaks specifically of the Spirit of 'sonship' (Rom. 8:15). As was customary in most primitive civilisations, the Roman Empire set a higher value on sons than daughters, so that, in the ranking of a Roman family, sons were automatically given favoured status. When Paul states that we have received the Spirit of sonship, he therefore indicates that God has placed 'most favoured status' upon us. We receive by faith in Christ the full measure of the favour of God that belonged to the Son of God by birthright. More than that, the same measure of adoptive status is applied to every believer, irrespective of nationality, generation or gender. While in the Roman or Jewish first-century family the daughters might be treated as second-class citizens, in the new adoptive family of God we all receive the Holy Spirit in the same measure. There are no second bests. Rather, as God's beloved children by adoption, men and women have an equal standing, both now and for all eternity.

Paul identifies two results of receiving the Spirit of sonship, both of which involve a kind of speaking. First, the inflow of the Spirit of adoption results in a new kind of verbal expression of intimacy with Father God.

> *But you received the Spirit of sonship. And by him we cry 'Abba, Father.'*
>
> Romans 8:15

> *God sent the Spirit of his Son into our hearts, the Spirit who calls out, 'Abba, Father.'*
>
> Galatians 4:6

The words Paul uses, 'cry' and 'call out', are both vigorous verbs. Demons 'cried out' when expelled by Jesus, people 'cried out' to Jesus for healing, the crowd 'cried out' for Jesus to be crucified, Jesus 'cried out' at the point of his death, and there will be 'a cry of joy' when the bridegroom comes at midnight. This clearly demonstrates that the first Christians were not in the habit of muttering or mumbling that God was their Father, in the casual repetition of an obligatory formula. Nor did they content themselves with silent reflection on the Fatherhood of God. Instead, their worship meetings were punctuated by enthusiastic outcries – 'Abba, Father!' Their new relationship with God as Father was not only intimate but also exuberant, an inner reality that at times could find noisy expression. Such intensity of feeling and fervour, overflowing in spontaneous cries of love, was not of human manufacture, nothing to do with mere religious excitement, for the source of these outcries was no less than the Spirit of God, the Spirit of adoption.

When Paul wrote to the Christians in Galatia and Rome, as usual he wrote his letter in Greek, the standard everyday language of the Empire. But when describing this spontaneous, Spirit-inspired cry to the Father, Paul uses the Aramaic word 'Abba'. So revolutionary, so remarkable did the first Christians find Jesus' invitation to know God as Father that they introduced a foreign word into their worship. Recognising that this privilege of intimacy with God was made possible only through Jesus Christ, Greek-speaking believers echoed their Saviour's own language in the Spirit-inspired cries that could be heard in their worship meetings.

Paul also records a second kind of speaking that results from the inflow of the Holy Spirit. Not only did the first Christians cry out to God as Abba, Father, but the Spirit of God also spoke to them, certainly through preaching and prophecy, but also inwardly, into the depths of their inner being:

> *The Spirit himself testifies with our spirit that we are God's children.*

> Romans 8:16

We can grow in confidence in the Christian faith in three distinct ways. First, we learn to take hold of the promises of Scripture: because I have put my trust in Christ as Saviour, these promises now apply to me. Second, we begin to be able to identify ways in which we have changed for the better since coming to faith. The third kind of Christian assurance is undoubtedly the highest – the inner testimony of the Holy Spirit. The customary theme of the Spirit's inner testimony speaks directly of the new status that has been granted us by faith in Christ: we have become nothing less than the adopted children of our Father God. There is a verse missing in most hymnbooks from Charles Wesley's great hymn 'And Can It Be', in which Wesley celebrates this inner, experiential witness of the Spirit to our salvation:

> *Still the small inward voice I hear,*
>   *That whispers all my sins forgiven;*
> *Still the atoning blood is near,*
>   *That quenched the wrath of hostile heaven:*
> *I feel the life his wounds impart;*
>   *I feel my Saviour in my heart.*

Many Western Christians have become wary of inner impressions and the intuitive, non-rational dimensions of living faith. Our instinctive fear is that such an emphasis could lead to a chaos of random impressions. While some certainly have made a habit of going overboard, no one could reasonably accuse the apostle Paul of anti-intellectualism, emotionalism, or frenzied hyper-subjectivism. The danger is that in rejecting extremism we have accidentally excluded a pivotal dimension of New Testament spirituality. We need to recover the discipline of listening to the inner voice of the Spirit, to learn again how to hear the Spirit of adoption witnessing to our spirit that we really are children of God. This is not the voice of aspiration – 'I do hope that I might be acceptable to God.' It is the divine voice of assurance – 'You are an adopted and beloved child of the Father in heaven. You really are.'

Personal reflection

The Spirit of adoption invites us to speak out our new status as beloved children of the Father, and to listen to the inner voice of promise as the Spirit assures us that we really do belong within the family of God. Have you ever taken an opportunity to call out to the Father or listen to the Spirit?

6

Revealing the Father to One Another

Faith in Christ opens up new possibilities of relationship both
with God and with other believers. When we are adopted by
God the Father, we receive a new family of brothers and
sisters in Christ. That's why Luke emphasises the committed
and supportive relationships of the early Church. The first
Christians prayed, broke bread and enjoyed meals together
(Acts 2:42–7). More than that, they made sure that no one
among them was left in material need (Acts 4:32–5). They were
discovering a new way of living, exploring in the freshness and
novelty of their new-born faith what it means to seek to live as
a 'colony of heaven' (Phil. 3:20, Moffatt's paraphrase).

The early Christians were both practical and affectionate.
Paul frequently encouraged believers to greet one another with
a holy kiss (Rom. 16:16; 1 Cor. 16:20; 2 Cor. 13:12; 1 Thess. 5:26).
The letters of the New Testament are littered with 'one another'
commands – be devoted to one another (Rom. 12:10); honour one
another (Rom. 12:10); live in harmony with one another
(Rom. 12:16); accept one another (Rom. 15:7); serve one another
(Gal. 5:13); bear with one another (Eph. 4:2); forgive one another
(Eph. 4:32); submit to one another (Eph. 5:21); teach and admonish
one another (Col. 3:16); encourage one another and build each
other up (1 Thess. 5:11); encourage one another (Heb. 3:13,

10:25); spur one another on (Heb. 10:24); live in harmony with one another (1 Pet. 3:8); offer hospitality to one another (1 Pet. 4:9), and so on.

Undergirding the rich variety of 'one another' commands is found the new commandment of Jesus: 'Love one another' (John 13:34). Peter placed great emphasis upon the love command: 'Love one another deeply, from the heart' (1 Pet. 1:22). The letters of John return to this command like an recurring refrain (1 John 3:11, 3:23, 4:7, 4:11, 4:12; 2 John 5). An ancient tradition tells that in John's last days of frail old age he had little strength to speak, but this one phrase remained constantly upon his lips: 'Little children, love one another.'

The trouble is that Christians can be so very difficult to love! We can be stubborn, self-opinionated, awkward, angular, troublemaking, wilful, divisive or just downright daft! This should come as no surprise: Christ died for sinners, not saints. Only those who cannot save themselves have need of a Saviour. Nonetheless, many Christians have reached a point of exasperation, whether with an individual, a group of believers or a whole church, when they feel that enough is enough – 'Surely the time has come to give up on these people!' And yet, we must insist, Jesus Christ has never given up on his Church. He sees the weaknesses, the self-indulgence, the half-heartedness so much more clearly than we ever could. His searching gaze is never misled by the glaze of religious respectability or by spiritual words that conceal a self-serving heart. And yet Christ loves the Church. If our Master has not given up on the Church, we have no right to cease from loving and serving. A time may come when it is appropriate to move from one church to another, but we should never give up loving *all* the people of God.

What's more, the Christ who sees the failings of his Church can see with equal clarity the failings of my life, in spirit and heart, in thoughts, motives and actions. And yet he is patient and merciful. If he were not, then I would be doomed, and the same is true for every believer, without exception. Since Christ is so full of grace towards me, and since I need nothing less than a vast measure of his abundant grace, then I need to relate to other Christians with an equivalent measure of grace, as generously as I can. Out of the abundance of Christ's patient love towards us, we must learn to walk in patience and in love alongside our fellow believers.

We have identified two motivations for loving the Church. First, we must love one another because of the plain commands of Christ and the New Testament. Second, we must love one another because we have discovered something of the enormity of the great and constant mercy that Christ has shown to each one of us. Here is a third motivation. We share as believers the most extraordinary privilege and task of showing the Father's love to one another, with the result that the manner in which we relate to one another will serve to strengthen or weaken each one's understanding of the Father's love.

Jesus reveals the Father's love, as do the Scriptures and the Holy Spirit. But if our natural disposition is negative, destructive, over-competitive, ever-complaining, over-demanding, perfectionist, gossiping or judgmental, we make it harder for other Christians to enjoy the Father's love. You know what it is like on a beach when someone settles next to you with a huge windbreak. By the time they have set it up, not a single ray of sun is able to penetrate the shadows it casts over a wide stretch of sand. In the same way, some Christians' negativity casts such broad shadows that no one near them is able to receive freely of the Father's love.

It is so easy for us to misunderstand someone's words or misread their intentions. It is so easy to nurse a grievance or keep a record of how others have let us down. When no one is perfect, fault-finding is easy. Like a dog with a bone, professional critics will not cease gnawing at their prey until every imperfection has been exposed to public display. Such follies may be the customary vice of those whose hearts are crabbed and sour. But there is no excuse for such destructive thoughts and poisoned tongues among those who claim the name of Christ. Isaiah expressed succinctly the attitude of the God of patient mercy to such accusatory vices, when he commanded in the name of the Lord that we must 'do away with the pointing finger and malicious talk' (Isa. 58:9). That means we need to eradicate such negativity entirely, immediately and permanently.

Here is a great responsibility for believers. Not only is the Father's character revealed through Jesus Christ. Not only is the Father's love brought to us by the presence of the Holy Spirit. But we have the remarkable opportunity to show the Father's love to one another, strengthening one another's confidence in the Father as we choose not to indulge the selfish and negative instincts of our sinful nature. We can easily make it difficult for others to walk tall in the love of the Father, but the alternative is so much more rewarding. As we learn to express the self-giving love of our heavenly Father, we strengthen the new family likeness and help one another grow in the intimacy and immensity of the Father's love.

Practical meditation

How can I help other believers develop a more positive image of God as Father? How can I show his love best to the people in my church I find it hardest to get along with?

7

Bible Meditation

THE PARABLE OF THE PRODIGAL SON – LUKE 15:11–24

Imagining with the son

In your imagination act out the role of the rebellious son. How does it feel to discover that your father has been looking out for your return? How does it feel when he embraces you? What does it mean to you when he rejects your suggestion that you assume the role of a servant and instead restores you to the full standing of a beloved son? Enter into the emotional contrast between making the journey home as a penitent and hearing your father announce a great party of restoration.

Imagining with the father

Now in your imagination enter into the role of the forgiving father. How does it feel when your son demands his inheritance without delay? How does it feel when you are hoping against hope for his return? What does it mean to you when you catch sight of a young man in the distance, with a start of recognition, a moment of hesitation in case you are mistaken, and then the certainty that this really is your own dear son coming home? Enter into the emotional contrast between seeing your son abandon you and the family home, and then your joyous announcement of his homecoming celebration.

Allow yourself to become absorbed into Jesus' story. As his words stimulate your imagination and stir your emotions, let these responses inform the way you relate to God as Father.

Poems, Prayers and Hymns for Reflection

PRAYER TO THE FATHER
Father, I abandon myself into your hands.
Do with me what you will,
Whatever you may do, I will thank you,
I am ready for all, I accept all.
Let only your will be done in me,
As in all your creatures,
I wish no more than this, O Lord.
Into your hands I commend my spirit;
I offer it to you with all the love of my heart,
For I love you, Lord, and so need to give myself,
To surrender myself into your hands
Without reserve and with boundless confidence
Because you are my Father.
Charles de Foucauld, 1858–1916

From MY WAY, MY LIFE, MY LIGHT
Behold the prodigal! To thee I come,
To hail my Father and to seek my home.
Nor refuge could I find, nor friend abroad,
Straying in vice and destitute of God.
O let thy terrors and my anguish end!
Be thou my refuge and be thou my friend:
Receive the son thou didst so long reprove,
Thou that art the God of love!
Matthew Prior, 1664–1721

LET US PRACTISE YOUR FORGIVENESS, LORD
O holy Jesus who didst for us die,
And on the altar bleeding lie,
Bearing all torment, pain, reproach and shame,
That we by virtue of the same,
Though enemies to God, might be
Redeemed, and set at liberty.
As thou didst us forgive,
So meekly let us love to others show,
And live in heaven on earth below.
Thomas Traherne, 1637–74

Be thou my vision, O Lord of my heart;
Naught be all else to me, save that thou art;
Thou my best thought, by day or by night,
Waking or sleeping, thy presence my light.

Be thou my wisdom, thou my true word;
I ever with thee, thou with me, Lord;
Thou my great Father, I thy true son;
Thou in me dwelling, and I with thee one.

Be thou my battle-shield, sword for the fight;
Be thou my dignity, thou my delight,
Thou my soul's shelter, thou my high tower:
Raise thou me heavenward, O power of my power.

Riches I heed not, nor man's empty praise;
Thou mine inheritance, now and always:
Thou and thou only, first in my heart,
High King of heaven, my treasure thou art.

High King of heaven, after victory is won,
May I reach heaven's joys, O bright heaven's Sun!
Heart of my own heart, whatever befall,
Still be my vision, O Ruler of all.

Ancient Irish
translated Mary Byrne 1880–1931
and Eleanor Hull 1860–1935

A hymn by Charles Wesley

This glorious, prolonged celebration of privileges of grace in Christ was written by Wesley to be used on the anniversary of our personal conversion. From its vast number of verses one of the most popular evangelical hymns has been extracted – 'O for a thousand tongues'. A much longer selection of Wesley's verses is provided here. It is undoubtedly too long to sing in full in public worship, but still has much to offer when read aloud or even sung in personal prayer.

Glory to God, and praise, and love
Be ever, ever given,
By saints below, and saints above,
The church in earth and heaven.

On this glad day the glorious Sun
Of righteousness arose;
On my benighted soul he shone,
And filled it with repose.

Sudden expired the legal strife;
'Twas then I ceased to grieve;
My second, real, living life
I then began to live.

Then with my heart I first believed,
Believed with faith divine;
Power with the Holy Ghost received
To call the Saviour mine.

I felt my Lord's atoning blood
Close to *my* soul applied;
Me, me he loved – the Son of God
For *me*, for *me* he died!

I found, and owned his promise true,
Ascertained of my part;
My pardon passed in heaven I knew,
When written on my heart.

O for a thousand tongues to sing
My dear Redeemer's praise!
The glories of my God and King,
The triumphs of his grace.

My gracious Master, and my God,
Assist me to proclaim,
To spread through all the earth abroad
The honours of thy name.

Jesus, the name that charms our fears,
That bids our sorrows cease;
'Tis music in the sinner's ears,
'Tis life, and health, and peace!

He breaks the power of cancelled sin,
He sets the prisoner free;
His blood can make the foulest clean,
His blood availed for me.

He speaks; and, listening to his voice,
New life the dead receive,
The mournful, broken hearts rejoice,
The humble poor believe.

Hear him, ye deaf; his praise, ye dumb,
Your loosened tongues employ;
Ye blind, behold your Saviour come;
And leap, ye lame, for joy.

Look unto him, ye nations; own
Your God, ye fallen race!
Look, and be saved through faith alone;
Be justified by grace!

See all your sins on Jesus laid;
The Lamb of God was slain,
His soul was once an offering made
For every soul of man.

Harlots, and publicans, and thieves
In holy triumph join;
Saved is the sinner that believes
From crimes as great as mine.

Murderers, and all ye hellish crew,
Ye sons of lust and pride,
Believe the Saviour died for you;
For me the Saviour died.

With me, your chief, you then shall know,
Shall feel your sins forgiven;
Anticipate your heaven below,
And own that love is heaven.

CHAPTER II

BEING WITH GOD

Stillness in the divine presence

God moves in a mysterious way
His wonders to perform;
He plants his footsteps in the sea,
And rides upon the storm.

Deep in unfathomable mines
Of never-failing skill,
He treasures up his bright designs
And works his sovereign will.

Ye fearful saints, fresh courage take,
The clouds ye so much dread
Are big with mercy, and shall break
In blessings on your head.

Judge not the Lord by feeble sense,
But trust him for his grace:
Behind a frowning providence
He hides a smiling face.

His purposes will ripen fast,
Unfolding every hour:
The bud may have a bitter taste,
But sweet will be the flower.

Blind unbelief is sure to err,
And scan his work in vain:
God is his own interpreter,
And he will make it plain.

William Cowper

1

Freedom in Relationship

Bookshops throughout the Western world teem with books on making the most of personal relationships. Despite the endless torrent of advice, no one can really tell us how to fall in love or how to stay in love. The way that two people discover that they love one another, how it feels for them to be in love, and their personal ways of expressing love's tenderness, in all these experiences there will be a unique dimension to any couple's relationship.

While every loving relationship is unique, several factors inevitably shape the way we relate. This is true of friendships, marriage and also relating to God. First, there is the impact of our culture. Here I am using the term 'culture' not in the sense of high culture, the world of Shakespeare and the opera, but rather in the sense of the conventions of everyday living – 'the way we do things round here'.

When I used to be a publisher, on my first visit to the Frankfurt Book Fair I walked down an aisle where German publishers of Christian books had their stands. As I passed each stand, the publishers came out to greet me, and shook my hand. Some also clicked their heels and crisply nodded their heads, which I did find slightly disconcerting, but my instinctive reaction was positive, impressed by this warmth of greeting. The next day I walked down the same aisle, and out came the German publishers to repeat the welcome. This was more than enough pressing of the flesh for me, and so I resolved not to go down that particular aisle more often than was strictly necessary!

Here we see a small instance of culture clash. For many Germans, a handshake is the customary greeting for everyone at their workplace each morning. For many Brits, a handshake is usually appropriate among colleagues to welcome someone to the firm, to congratulate them on a promotion or to wish them well when they retire, move to another firm, or are made redundant. Not only does British culture tend to be more informal than German culture, but most of us inhabit a 'don't touch me' world. A Brit can easily misinterpret the first German handshake as expressing a warm greeting, when for a German it is really no more nor less than an obligatory formality.

Just as our culture shapes the ways we build relationships, whether in business or in romance, our temperament also makes a huge difference. I remember two friends at university who were polar opposites. Colin explained to me that his idea of a perfect evening with friends was to sit in silence, doing nothing, saying nothing, but simply enjoying being together. David, meanwhile, was a natural-born party-goer. If there was a disco on campus, he would be there. If David was in a room, conversation would be sure to flow. For Colin, friendship meant quietness and stillness: for David, a riot of laughter and noise. While it would hardly be easy for such contrasting characters to cultivate a friendship that both could understand, let alone enjoy, we certainly could not fairly conclude that only one of them was friendly. Close relationships are expressed in many different ways, and it would be sheer folly to impose one style of friendship upon everyone. In a similar way, our temperaments critically determine the ways of praying that will come to us most naturally and in which we will be able to express ourselves most fully.

The third great factor that shapes the way we relate to God is the sub-cultural style of our denomination and local church. Because I came to faith in an Anglican setting, the first time I saw the little glasses that Baptists traditionally use for communion I thought they looked decidedly bizarre. The first time many Baptists attend a communion with a common cup their disquiet is often more hygienic than aesthetic, wondering how anyone ever escapes if a noxious virus visits someone in such a congregation! Denominations and local churches tend to develop conventions in prayer, certain methods and postures, styles and tones of voice that are normative. The familiar is valued as beneficial and authentically spiritual. Therefore we all tend to look askance at the unfamiliar, which at best may seem rather strange or eccentric, at worst alien, extremist or contrived.

These conventions can be found in every kind of church setting. I remember hearing a Pentecostal pastor bring a prophetic word of gentle comfort and encouragement. His tradition made a close connection between spiritual anointing and high decibels, and so the gentle words were declaimed in resounding tones that would have won first prize at a convention of town criers. Within the culture, the shouting indicated holy unction. Outside the culture it seemed strident, aggressive and awkwardly at odds with the content of the prophetic utterance.

Similarly, I attended a new church prayer gathering, in a stream that is renowned for its upbeat emphasis on vision and advance. Everyone was invited to pray vigorously for accelerating church growth and for mega-churches to be established wherever this particular stream is working. I noticed, sitting beside me, a couple who began weeping, and I asked them what was going on. They explained that they were working as pioneer missionaries in an unresponsive country, where they had not seen anyone come to faith in several years of patient service. The culturally acceptable mode of praying was urgent and insistent, always looking for triumph and imminent advance. This couple needed prayer with a different tempo, for they were investing long term in showing the love of Jesus. They had become seed for the gospel, but before they could bear much fruit there was a difficult path to follow, for their seed had first to be buried in the ground and die (John 12:24). Short-term triumphalism can become insensitive or dismissive of the virtues of persistence, steadfastness and long-term self-sacrifice.

Sometimes in the historic denominations we have conformed to a different cultural norm. While some kneel and some sit for prayer, the solemn and sonorous monotone and the predictable and often vacuous content of public prayer convey a clear message: proper prayer is formal and boring, a ritual to be endured, a compulsory and purgatorial activity, without any expected impact or discernible consequences, either for those for whom we pray or for those engaging in such routine acts of religiosity. I must confess that, as a teenager, I found the call to prayer in Sunday services an almost instantaneous cure for insomnia. Going through the motions of praying has won for itself its very own alternative beatitude: Blessed are they who expect little, for they shall not be disappointed.

The impact of culture can lead to considerable misunderstanding among Christians. At one conference I invited people to identify aspects of prayer they found particularly rewarding. One woman from India described the way that she loved flowers, spending time arranging and painting them. She explained that sometimes she would take a beautiful flower in her hands and meditate upon its beauty, and this would lead her into taking delight in the Creator God, inspired by such extravagant and delicate floral artistry. Many of those present were intrigued and attracted by this novel approach to prayer, but another Indian woman was clearly distressed. She explained that in her part of India the Hindus were the dominant religious grouping and frequently used flowers in their idol worship. Therefore, she concluded, Christians could never use flowers in prayer, since flowers are inextricably linked with Hinduism.

Here was the power of culture in action. It could well be that this particular woman would never be able to use flowers as an aid to prayer, and she needed to know that she was absolutely free to make such a choice. What she was tempted to do, however, was to absolutise the values of her cultural setting, with the suggestion that any use of flowers in prayer was unavoidably and intrinsically Hindu, and therefore absolutely incompatible with Christian praying. Just as we must be careful to avoid syncretism – an unconscious captivity to the prevailing non-Christian cultural context – we must also be careful to avoid cultural imperialism – absolutising the ways of praying customary within our local church or denomination to the exclusion of experimentation and learning from others. There is a great danger that we become captive to the sub-culture of our denomination or local church, incapable of benefiting from unfamiliar aspects of prayer that have the potential greatly to enrich our personal walk with God.

When it comes to relating to God, we cannot reasonably impose a single, rigid method on how different people pray. What is required is never a fixed formula – this works for me, so it must work for you! Instead, we need to discover the freedom to experiment and explore what it means to spend time being with God. The guiding principle behind this little book is that many things will be suggested, but none will be imposed. The borders of your cultural comfort zones may be breached, but the invitation to journey into unexplored territory is always an opportunity, never an obligation.

Pause for thought

Identify two or three aspects of prayer that are familiar in your Christian culture. Are there any that tend to be neglected, avoided or even distrusted?

2

Posture and Body Language

Anyone involved in pastoral counselling is familiar with the power of body language. Someone may control their words and tone of voice to conceal how they really feel, but the secrets of our inner life are often unmasked by the details of our posture. It is not only the client's posture that is important. The counsellor's posture will influence the tone of the session. This is true not only at the beginning, when the client needs to be put at ease. Just as important is the way that posture conveys our inner response when something confidential is shared. If the counsellor's body language conveys distance, formality or a negative reaction, many clients will quickly switch from vulnerability to defensiveness. Their posture may in turn indicate that their defences have gone back up, behind folded arms or crossed legs.

It is not just in counselling that body language is significant. In fact, this kind of communication is only relevant in the relatively unusual and specialised context of counselling because body language is an integral and habitual part of everyday life. Human communication skills are non-verbal as well as verbal. Sometimes the non-verbal dimension serves to reinforce the message of our words, not only in the gestures of a preacher or politician, but in ordinary conversations and business negotiations. Some non-verbal communication is not so much to emphasise our words as to add a distinctive reinforcement to their persuasiveness: a tall person may stand close to someone shorter to assert their authority; we may make eye contact to appeal for assent; we may lean forward to express our involvement in the conversation or a desire to clinch our case.

Still other postures and gestures neither act out nor reinforce our words, but function as part of a quite distinct non-verbal conversation, a kind of relational dance of approval and disapproval, friendship and affection, distrust and suspicion. Someone skilled at interpreting unconscious gestures can spot the first hints of sexual attraction before the couple involved are even aware of it themselves. We often have no idea that we are communicating and relating non-verbally, but although we do not consciously decode the gestures of others, our brains are programmed to express and to receive and interpret a rich and subtle vocabulary of gesture. Whenever we are with other people, we relate and communicate not only through our words but also with our bodies.

The rich, instinctive vocabulary of non-verbal communication raises important questions about prayer. If our words are normally strengthened by gestures, and if our body language is an integral part of our relating to others, then can our bodies enrich the way we pray? Much Western praying has traditionally rejected this suggestion. In many churches there is only one approved posture for prayer, usually either kneeling or sitting with eyes closed. Kneeling is certainly an eloquent expression of some aspects of our relationship with God, notably humility and surrender. It probably echoes the homage paid to a medieval lord, acknowledging his authority and declaring dedicated allegiance. Kneeling does, however, have one significant disadvantage: most of us are only able to stay on our knees for a very limited period of time.

A far more restrictive and less expressive posture is adopted whenever people choose to hunch forward in their seats. This posture may once have had a calculated ambiguity, suggesting to the critical onlooker that you might perhaps have been kneeling after all. In the pattern of church culture, this hunched posture has often become normative and instinctive – part of 'the way we do things round here'. Newcomers quickly copy this posture as part of the non-verbal vocabulary of the Christian life. In many churches, whether on Sundays, in house groups or at any other kind of meeting, the invitation to pray is immediately followed by the sight of Christians leaning forward and hunching up.

The 'prayer hunch' is an extremely unsatisfactory posture. The body language is extremely closed and defensive, by implication both to others in the room and towards God. The posture even appears to be semi-foetal, turned in on itself and probably restricting the circulation. If in any other kind of conversation someone adopted this posture with the same suddenness with which it follows an invitation to pray, many would reasonably assume that the hunched one was deeply traumatised or in need of first aid!

So why do so many Christians instinctively adopt 'the hunch of prayer'? My own suspicion is that the ultimate accusation must be laid against the insidious, pervasive and yet hidden influence of Platonism. For much of its history the Church in the West has been unconsciously captive to Platonic presuppositions. Platonism was essentially dualistic, dividing humanity's higher nature, our spirituality and rationality, from our lower nature, our bodily existence and its mortality. Within a Platonic framework it is assumed that, in order to express our spirit as fully as possible, the best thing we can do with our physical body is to get it out of the way. The body is parked, switched off or neutralised in order to free the spirit for the higher activity of prayer, to which the body is entirely unable to make a positive contribution.

Such a negative understanding of our material existence is alien to classical Judaeo-Christian thinking. In creation we were fashioned as integral beings, body and spirit intertwined. Beyond this life, while we will be freed from mortality and sinfulness we do not face the prospect of becoming disembodied spirits, for our eternal salvation will not be complete without the provision of replacement, resurrection bodies. To be sure, the apostle Paul speaks of an inner conflict in the Christian between flesh and spirit, which has led some to suppose that Christian spirituality is indifferent or hostile to bodily existence. However, it is vital to understand that when Paul uses the word flesh (*sarx*) he does not mean our physicality, our bodies, for which he uses the word *soma*. The 'flesh' in Pauline terminology is used to convey his conviction that the essential problem of the human condition is to be found not in our bodies, but in our characters. Paul's term, *sarx*, is rightly understood to signify our sinful nature, not our material existence.

Once we escape the prejudices of Platonic dualism and the tyranny of a church culture that excludes non-verbal communication from the life of prayer, new possibilities begin to open before us. When we pray to God with words, we can reinforce our communication with the emphatic and subtle language of gesture. More than that, since our non-verbal skills of communication are a gift from the Creator that enrich our capacity for deepening relationships, we can also explore praying beyond words, when our posture not only enhances but actually becomes a means of expressing our prayer.

A good starting point for personal experiment is a posture often recommended in counselling. This is a way to take charge of your body language, so that your posture expresses an active choice of right relationship with the God of love. Find a comfortable chair, and sit reasonably upright but not too stiff. Choose to express openness with your whole posture, with arms and legs relaxed and not crossed. It may help to hold out your hands, palms up, or rest them on your legs. Don't let your hands become taut or clenched. Rather than having your head drop forwards, which usually indicates exhaustion, either sit as if talking to someone across the room or lift your head slightly, in order to express thankfulness, praise and also a willingness to receive anew of God's presence and love. If you hate this posture, you need never try it. But I certainly find it much more rewarding and expressive that the curled-up constrictions of the conventional 'hunch of prayer'!

Pause for thought

Consider how your body language is a natural part of communicating and relating to others. Is your body language expressive or switched off when you seek to communicate with God?

3

Prayer that Relieves Tension

Whatever we are feeling keenly tends to show in our bodies. Too much tension, and our shoulders get stiff. In worse cases, the stress may begin to show in stomach cramps or an ulcer, high blood pressure or even a heart attack. Some people become walking knots of tension: stress is etched deeply upon their hands, face and posture.

A simple but rewarding way of using our bodies to express non-verbal prayer is what Richard Foster has called the hands down, hands up prayer. The underlying insight is that sometimes when we turn to prayer our lives are so filled with anxieties, pressure and stress that we have little or no space into which we can receive from God. We are like a Christmas shopper so laden down with purchases that we could not even receive a free gift on the way out of a department store.

There really is no need to pray through gritted teeth whenever we become knotted up on the inside. Rather than praying for a few fleeting moments before returning to the 'things I just can't leave at the moment', we can choose to hand over our pressures before the Father. Hold out your hands with the palms facing downwards and name the concerns that you want to release. As you name them, make a conscious effort to let them go, giving them into the care of God. The physical gesture is a way of enacting a biblical principle: 'Cast all your anxiety on him because he cares for you' (1 Pet. 5:7).

Once your cares have been handed over, you are ready for stage two. Turn your hands so that the palms are face up, symbolising the fact that you have made space to receive from God. Then pray something like this: 'Father, I am now able to come to you with empty hands. Please give me a fresh gift of your love and your peace.' In times of pressure, the discipline of the hands down, hands up prayer is a great way of choosing release rather than getting locked up in stress. For me, it has certainly proven on many occasions to be a successful means of release and relaxation through prayer.

Practical experiment

A more complex way of expressing tension and release involves reading aloud a prayer while acting it out with your hands. Here is an example of such a prayer with which you might like to experiment. Try letting each phrase function as a stage direction, expressing the hidden feelings of your heart through the non-verbal eloquence of your fingers.

Lord, my hands are clenched so tightly, I am grasping my life,
    refusing to give it,
My knuckles are whitening with the strain of it,
But I won't let go.
In my tightly clenched fist
I hold all of my life,
The things I don't want others to see:
I hold my pride, my desire to appear right,
My desire to appear strong;
I hold my anxieties, my fear that I won't be accepted as I am;
I hold my anger, my protection

Against anyone who comes too close to my secret.
My arms ache with the tension,
The immense energy required to hide myself from myself,
From my brothers and sisters,
From you, Lord.
To lash out against my brother or sister,
And against you, Lord.

Lord, as I slowly, painfully open my hands,
I offer to you all they have been grasping so tightly,
I offer to you the fear of being known as I am,
I offer to you the fear of my offering being rejected,
I offer to you the anger, the defences I use to protect myself,
I offer to you the hurt for the times
I have offered myself and have been rejected.

Lord, my hands can move again!
They can stretch and wiggle!
They can clap and dance!
They can touch and feel!
They can reach out and heal!

Lord, with these hands you have freed
I reach out to my brothers and sisters,
Let my hands be your hands,
Let them be gentle messengers of forgiveness and peace,
Let them be strong assurances of support,
Let them be the sign of your promise to us.

Source unknown

4

Creativity before God

A rich variety of postures can enhance and express different kinds of prayer. In the New Testament, the only posture specifically recommended is 'raising holy hands' (1 Tim. 2:8). While some prefer to think that this is a metaphorical reference to hands, it is much more likely to be a literal description of a physical expression of prayer. In the Old Testament there is a huge catalogue of postures. For example, people pray while standing, sitting, walking, marching, and lying prostrate on the ground.

Sometimes at prayer workshops I have invited people to describe and then demonstrate the postures for prayer that they use themselves or that are familiar in their home church. This has proven particularly rewarding at the London Institute for Contemporary Christianity, where the course members are from many different countries, because the rich variety of postures produces a creative clash of cultures. I have seen Indians kneel with palms down on the floor and head bowed in a way deeply expressive of humility; Nigerians showing others how to pray lying face down on the ground – sometimes to the astonishment of North Americans who have never seen anyone assume such a posture, except perhaps a drunk; Danes raising a decorous hand in prayer; and Ugandans striding vigorously about a building while praying for the victorious advance of the Church.

In addition to these postures that most of us are quite capable of exploring if we so desire, a privileged minority are gifted to express their prayers through dance and mime. I am personally a great believer in the ministry of dance, so long as I don't have to dance myself! It has been a privilege to encourage those with the gift to express prayer in this way: the positive impact for a congregation is often immense. As for anyone trying to encourage me to dance personally, I happen to think that there are few things less edifying than an overweight preacher, with minimal co-ordination of the limbs, performing a stumbling jig on a platform! Not everyone is gifted and called to be a David of the dance.

While compulsory dance would be a nightmare for some, the Church has usually tended to the opposite extreme. I remember vividly a student who was studying dance who came to see me to discuss a problem with prayer. 'My concern,' she explained, 'is that I often express my prayers by dancing before the Lord, and I just wanted to check whether this was OK.' It was, of course, far from OK. It was absolutely marvellous! Her ability was God-given and she was able to give expression to the deepest convictions, hopes and concerns of her inmost being through the medium of dance with far greater eloquence and subtlety than ever she could find with words.

For those of us who are more leaden-limbed, walking can be a great accompaniment to prayer. When pastoring one church I set aside a day of prayer each month. If I had tried to pray all day while sitting down I would very soon have needed to fight off the temptation to drift into dozing. Instead, I went out into the countryside and prayed while striding down country lanes. In this way I was able to enjoy the beauty of creation while praying systematically through the needs of the people of the church. Only while walking could I have kept on praying for so long. I therefore make this practical suggestion: even within your living room or bedroom, if you can't concentrate on prayer while sitting down and if lying down deals a death blow to consciousness, try getting up on your feet to march your prayers to heaven!

Just as having fellow Christians display prayer postures that they find profitable can surprise us, provoking us to experiment beyond the often narrow limits of our own familiar and habitual range, it can also be rewarding to encourage people both to list and to demonstrate constructive ways of expressing prayer in words. Some Christians are absolutely convinced that set prayers can only be stifling, and so it is a pleasant surprise for them to discover that others find this kind of prayer rewarding. Others are only used to a very formal style of public prayer, in which no one ever raises their voice. For such Christians it can be startling to discover that others walk or march as they pray, clap as they pray, sound instruments or wave banners as they pray.

Some Christians still come from a denominational culture where the very thought of praying in tongues seems at best eccentric, at worst positively dangerous. It can be very instructive for such believers to discover that someone from another church, who seems to them a perfectly reasonable individual and a clearly committed Christian, actually finds it beneficial to speak in tongues.

One of the biggest shocks comes when many Western Christians first encounter the practice of everyone praying aloud simultaneously. For some, to speak at the same time as others seems quite alien, peculiar and even ill-mannered, with the sole exception of a set prayer, such as the Lord's Prayer. For others, it is a perfectly natural and habitual style of prayer for everyone to cry aloud to the Lord about a particular theme, at the same time and in their own words.

Whether with a variety of postures or different ways of verbalising prayer, the same principle applies. It can do us good to be lifted out of our familiar cultural rut as we discover the rich variety of ways in which our fellow believers express prayer. The key is to stay focused on what ultimately matters: not the means of communication, verbal or bodily, but rather the object of our prayers, the God and Father of our Lord Jesus Christ.

Practical application

Try experimenting with a posture or a way of verbalising prayer with which you are unfamiliar.

5

Biblical Meditation

Just as our praying can be enriched by exploring physical expressions and enhancements of whatever we want to communicate, there is also a place for the cultivation of creative inactivity. A well-trodden path into stillness before God is found through meditation, but a vital contrast must immediately be emphasised between biblical and eastern meditation. The eastern forms of meditation have their roots in Hinduism and Buddhism. They are often expressed in a less overtly religious form in many yoga classes and New Age influenced stress-relief programmes. The essence of such meditation is self-emptying. For many over-stressed Westerners, on the treadmill of excessive working hours, over-tight deadlines and impossible expectations, the prospect of losing oneself in an oblivion, where the clamouring demands of modern life are finally subdued and silenced, seems very attractive. It appears to promise a kind of heaven, a liberation into serenity without the hazards of tranquiliser addiction or alcohol abuse.

From the Christian perspective, there are two critical objections to this meditative oblivion, one theological and one anthropological. Theologically, the Christian understanding of the spiritual dimensions of human existence recognises not only the possibility of encounter with God, by his Holy Spirit, but also the operation of malevolent spirits, forces of darkness that can have a desperately damaging impact upon the human psyche. Uncritical self-emptying and openness to the spiritual dimensions beyond material existence will always run the risk of a Faustian bargain, in which temporary release from bondage to stress comes with the hidden price tag of an enduring bondage of the soul.

The anthropological objection concerns the essence of what it is to be human. While the Buddhist aspires to the ultimate Nirvana of nothingness which entails the extinction or absorption of individual consciousness, the Christian understanding is that men and women are created as relational beings. Made in the image of the triune God, who enjoys eternal relationships of pure love between the three persons of the Godhead, we discover and develop our true selves and fulfil our inner potential not through the dissolution of individual consciousness but rather in the exploration of loving encounter with the God of love. To be sure, Christian meditation also includes entering into a liberation from the cares and stresses of life. But the higher dimensions of human existence, beyond the treadmill of daily duties, are not to be discovered in the oblivion of self but rather in the re-centring of self in relationship with God.

Biblical meditation provides many gateways through which we can explore the cultivation of this relationship with God that lies at the very heart of human existence. With a doctrinal, abstract passage or verse, there is much benefit from taking time to chew over the words and concepts; memorising often helps. Just as a succulent sirloin of steak is best eaten slowly if it is to be enjoyed to the full, biblical meditation seeks to slow down our reading to a snail's pace. Some find it beneficial to repeat a verse several times, placing the dominant stress on each word or phrase in turn. In this way, the full weight of meaning is gradually unfolded and grasped:

> *Christ* died for the ungodly.
> Christ *died* for the ungodly.
> Christ died *for the ungodly.*
>
> Romans 5:6

With narrative passages, we can learn to enter imaginatively into the passage, allowing God to speak to us through the character with whom we are seeking to identify. At this level, biblical meditation is no longer exclusively conceptual, but also imaginative, as we allow our minds to be seized by the events and emotions of the biblical text. Phil, a church leader, told me about his experience of this kind of biblical meditation on a supervised retreat. Phil had decided to take this time out because he felt spiritually dry, worn out by the demands of being a 'professional' Christian. On the first morning Phil's spiritual advisor gave him the story of Peter's restoration by the risen Christ (John 21:15–23). Phil reported back at lunch-time with an abstract analysis of the major theological issues raised by the passage. His advisor passed no comment on Phil's insights, but sent him away for the afternoon with the same passage, and an invitation to read more deeply.

In the afternoon, Phil turned from abstract theology to exploring how he might preach from the passage. Freed from the normal pastoral and administrative responsibilities of his working week, his mind was feeling particularly fertile. At supper-time, Phil presented his advisor with two very acceptable sermon outlines. Once again his advisor passed no comment, but sent Phil away with the same passage and an invitation to read more deeply.

This repetition was beginning to frustrate Phil. He began to fear that his advisor had a less than satisfactory knowledge of the Bible if he could recommend only one passage for meditation. Not wanting to cause trouble, Phil considered the passage a third time and began to discover insights into Jesus' methods of pastoral care. Phil was excited by Jesus' patience, thoroughness and personal touch. He also recognised that Jesus granted Peter an experiential assurance that he was truly forgiven and restored by giving him another chance to serve his Master, despite his threefold denial. Phil's advisor did not respond to his insights into pastoral methodology. Once again he sent him away to reflect on the same passage.

This time Phil was really stumped. He had brought his best efforts and professional expertise to the passage. In theological analysis, sermon outlines and pastoral application he had garnered the best insights he possibly could. But the clear implication of his advisor's silence was that he was missing the point. What on earth was left to achieve? If his best efforts were to no avail, perhaps he should not have bothered to come on the retreat in the first place. With great reluctance, he turned to the passage again.

In the previous sessions Phil had come to the Bible well-armoured with his professional skills. This time he read the passage feeling thoroughly fed up and frustrated, with nothing left to offer. Then something new began to happen. Instead of reading the passage at arm's length, in the safety of detached analysis, he began to enter into it imaginatively. His own sense of failure allowed him to begin to enter into Peter's failure. Now the risen Christ was no longer only bringing restoration to an apostle nearly two thousand years ago. As Phil identified with Peter in his failure, the risen Christ met with him through the biblical narrative, in an encounter that renewed his sense of call to ministry and released him into a fresh and intimate surrender before his risen Lord. Biblical meditation brought Phil to a place of humility, where Christ could truly restore his soul.

Self-evaluation

Are there times when you read the Bible 'at arm's length', not allowing the Scriptures to speak directly into your own life and walk with God?

6

From Meditation to Contemplation

In biblical meditation we can learn the discipline of focus and surrender, where the everyday pressures and demands of life are left on one side. Beyond meditation we can enter the arena of contemplation, where we are no longer thinking about God or bringing our praise and requests before the divine throne. Here we come to the place of stillness, beyond adoration and intercession, where we begin to learn simply to be with God. The cultivation of the divine presence is where contemplative prayer begins.

Although there are many spiritual classics rich with insights into the discipline and art of contemplative prayer, those unfamiliar with this way of praying usually find it helpful to begin with the Bible. We will therefore consider two psalms where particularly suggestive metaphors open the way to stillness in the presence. In both cases, a key statement is made twice. To late-twentieth-century Western readers, such repetition may seem superfluous. But repetition in the poet's art is no mere self-indulgence from a more leisurely age. The metaphor's repetition is designed quite deliberately to slow down the reader.

> *I wait for the Lord, my soul waits,*
> *and in his Word I put my hope.*
> *My soul waits for the Lord*

> *more than watchmen wait for the morning,*
> *more than watchmen wait for the morning.*
>   Psalm 130:5–6

> *I have stilled and quietened my soul;*
> *like a weaned child with its mother,*
> *like a weaned child is my soul within me.*
>   Psalm 131:2

Many people today feel constantly hard-pressed for time and so we become speed readers, flicking through the pages with urgent haste. We consume books in a rush, as literary fast food. Just as a hiker will pause to drink in a glorious view, the psalmist invites us not only to read at walking pace, but even to pause for a while in order to drink in the divine presence. The psalmist's crafted repetition is no slip of the pen, but rather an invitation to dwell on the reinforced metaphor, discovering for ourselves its implications for our praying.

Turning first to Psalm 130, the movement of prayer in these two verses is expressed in the verb 'to wait', which occurs five times. Here is no rushing into prayer. The psalmist is seeking not merely to acknowledge the fact of divine omnipresence but to embrace the deeper reality of the perceived presence. This attentive waiting, to use Brother Lawrence's delightful phrase, is part of the art and discipline of 'practising the presence of God'.

Three times the psalmist reports his waiting upon God – I wait, my soul waits (x2). While this repetition is emphatic, the psalmist has not yet engaged the imagination of the reader in the experience of waiting. This comes about in the twice-stated metaphor of the watchmen, which is designed to provoke three kinds of question. Conceptually, how does a watchman wait for morning? Imaginatively, what does it feel like to be waiting for the dawn? Comparatively, what might this suggest about prayerful waiting for the divine presence?

For a watchman in the ancient world, dawn was anticipated as the time of safety, when the danger of enemy attack under the cover of darkness would have passed. The return of the sun is therefore awaited with a persistent eagerness. He would await with patience, since he could do nothing to hurry the sun's return, but also with confidence, since the sun had never failed to make its expected appearance. More than that, in the first light of dawn an ancient watchman would surely have experienced something of that sense of wonder that arises within the human spirit whenever we are up early enough, or late enough, to see the radiant birth of a new day.

The psalmist invites us to consider how a watchman waits, enter imaginatively into that experience, and then make creative comparisons with our prayerful waiting for God. Out of this meditation upon the watchman, we receive encouragement to bring the following qualities to our praying: attentiveness, persistence and eagerness, patience and confidence, and finally a growing sense of wonder at the dawning of his presence.

In Psalm 131 the psalmist invites us to still and quieten our soul before God, like a weaned child with its mother. There is a remarkable intimacy between mother and child. The baby knows the mother's voice and heartbeat even from within the womb. In the first days after birth, immature eyes have a limited range of focus, but a baby can already see the mother's face perfectly while feeding at her breast. Thus the baby quickly develops an intimate knowledge of the mother's face, the sound of her voice and the touch and fragrance of her skin.

Young babies who are greedy feeders may not settle easily in their mother's arms, for as soon as they smell the milk they begin to root around for another feed. A weaned infant has passed the stage of constantly demanding food, but is still young enough not to have outgrown or forgotten the pure pleasure of absolute security with their mum. It is unfailingly delightful to see the indecorous abandonment of a young child asleep in its mother's arms, limbs flopped and dangling casually, fully confident that the mother's love is devoted, protective, unfailing and available to be enjoyed. Here is one of those rare but striking moments in the Old Testament where the parental comparison to our relationship with God is motherly rather than fatherly. In this wonderfully evocative metaphor, the psalmist captures something of what it can mean to choose the way of abandoned stillness, leaving all cares and activity to one side, and learning to be at rest in contemplating the enormity and intensity of the love of God. If we want to begin to discover serenity in prayer, we need to learn to cultivate the way of stillness.

Sometimes we can try too hard in prayer. When we begin to enter this stillness, we discover a new perspective on the demands and stresses of life. We also gain a new perspective on prayer, for the stillness of contemplation takes us beyond the place of verbalised petitions as we enter the dimension of prayer where *being with God* becomes ultimately more important than *asking from God*. It would, however, be a mistake to think that contemplation can only be about stillness and tranquillity. Bernini's famous statue of Santa Teresa d'Avila expresses an extraordinary emotional intensity in marble, depicting the arrow of divine love about to be plunged into the heart of the ecstatic woman, altogether enraptured and overcome by an unforgettable encounter with the risen Christ. When she wrote of this experience, Teresa described a golden, flaming arrow that filled her with pain and yet infinite bliss. The statue is displayed in Santa Maria della Vittoria, a fairly modest church in Rome, and it evokes a lavish mystical fervour that has only been the experience of the privileged few. While admiring such rare, intense, even extravagant abandonment to divine love, we need to hear the psalmist's beckoning to every believer and discover more of the place of stillness. It takes time and discipline to learn first how to await the coming of God and then how to enjoy and remain at rest in the divine presence.

Practical application

How would you evaluate yourself when it comes to stillness before God?
- *a) impatient activist, keen to get on with doing and achieving*
- *b) too exhausted to be still without falling asleep*
- *c) inexperienced, but willing to try*
- *d) enjoying and growing in the art of contemplative prayer*

7

Bible Meditation

PSALMS 130 AND 131

Turn again to one of the psalms of contemplation we have been exploring (130, 131). Seek to set all other concerns on one side so that the living God becomes the sole focus of your attention. Stay with the psalm reflectively for as long as you can, entering into the metaphor of the watchman's patient waiting or the stillness and security of the weaned child in its mother's arms.

Poems, Prayers and Hymns for Reflection

Love's sweetest mark, laud's highest theme, man's most
desired light,
To love him life, to leave him death, to live in him delight.
He mine by gift, I his by debt, thus each to other due,
First friend he was, best friend he is, all times will try
him true.

Robert Southwell (1561–95)

Thou art my Life: if Thou but turn away,
My life's a thousand deaths: Thou art my Way;
Without Thee, Lord, I travel not, but stray.
My Light Thou art; without Thy glorious sight,
Mine eyes are darkened with perpetual night.
My God, Thou art my Way, my Life, my Light.
Thou art my Way; I wander, if Thou fly.
Thou art my Light; if hid, how blind am I!
Thou art my Life; if Thou withdraw, I die ...
Disclose Thy sunbeams; close Thy wings, and stay:
See, see how I am blind, and dead, and stray,
O Thou, that art my Light, my Life, my Way.

Francis Quarles (1592–1644)

From ST PATRICK'S BREASTPLATE
May the strength of God guide me this day, and may his power
preserve me.
May the wisdom of God instruct me; the eye of God watch
over me;
the ear of God hear me; the word of God give sweetness to
my speech;
the hand of God defend me; and may I follow the way
of God.
Christ be with me, Christ before me,
Christ be after me, Christ within me,
Christ beneath me, Christ above me,
Christ at my right hand, Christ at my left ...
Christ in every eye that sees me.
Christ in every ear that hears me ...
I bind unto myself the name, the strong name of the Trinity;
by invocation of the same, the Three in One and One
in Three,
of whom all nature has creation; Eternal Father, Spirit, Word;
praise to the Lord of my salvation,
salvation is of Christ the Lord.
(From the translation by C.F. Alexander)

O love that will not let me go,
I rest my weary soul in thee;
I give thee back the life I owe,
That in thine ocean depths its flow
May richer, fuller be.

O Light, that followest all my way,
I yield my flickering torch to thee;

My heart restores its borrowed ray,
That in thy sunshine's blaze its day
    May brighter, fairer be.

O Joy, that seekest me through pain,
    I cannot close my heart to thee;
I trace the rainbow through the rain,
    And feel the promise is not vain
    That morn shall tearless be.

O Cross, that liftest up my head,
    I dare not ask to fly from thee;
I lay in dust life's glory dead,
And from the ground there blossoms red
    Life that shall endless be.
                    George Matheson, 1842–1906

A hymn by Charles Wesley

O love divine, how sweet thou art!
When shall I find my willing heart
    All taken up by thee?
I thirst, and faint, and die to prove
The greatness of redeeming love,
    The love of Christ to me.

Stronger his love than death or hell;
    Its riches are unsearchable;
    The first-born sons of light
Desire in vain its depths to see,
They cannot reach the mystery,
The length, and breadth, and height.

God only knows the love of God;
O that it now were shed abroad
In this poor stony heart!
For love I sigh, for love I pine:
This only portion, Lord, be mine,
Be mine this better part.

O that I could for ever sit,
With Mary at the Master's feet!
Be this my happy choice,
My only care, delight, and bliss,
My joy, my heaven on earth be this
To hear the Bridegroom's voice.

O that I could with favoured John
Recline my weary head upon
The dear Redeemer's breast!
From care, and sin, and sorrow free,
Give me, O Lord, to find in thee
My everlasting rest.

Thy only love do I require,
Nothing in earth beneath desire,
Nothing in heaven above;
Let earth, and heaven, and all things go,
Give me thy only love to know,
Give me thy only love.

CHAPTER III

THE HOLY PRESENCE

Sinfulness, confession and the cross

There is a fountain filled with blood
Drawn from Immanuel's veins;
And sinners plunged beneath that flood
Lose all their guilty stains.

The dying thief rejoiced to see
That fountain in his day;
And there may I, though vile as he,
Wash all my sins away.

Dear dying Lamb, thy precious blood
Shall never lose its power,
Till all the ransomed church of God
Be saved, to sin no more.

E'er since, by faith, I saw the stream
Thy flowing wounds supply,
Redeeming love has been my theme,
And shall be till I die.

Then in a nobler, sweeter song
I'll sing thy power to save,
When this poor lisping, stammering tongue
Lies silent in the grave.

William Cowper

1

Status and Process

When I arrive back at Heathrow from a trip overseas, my British citizenship speeds me through airport security. I am not asked how often I sang the national anthem while abroad, or whether I can recite in chronological order the names of the kings and queens of the United Kingdom. My passport decrees a status that is unchangeable and beyond dispute. In the same way, once justified by faith in Christ, my status before the Father is settled. The condition of every single person who has put their trust in Christ is equal and secure: we are justified by faith in him.

Confidence before God through faith in Christ has been famously celebrated by Charles Wesley:

> *Bold I approach the eternal throne*
> *And claim the crown through Christ my own.*

Is such boldness legitimate and appropriate, or was Wesley carried away by his own rhetoric, cultivating an arrogant attitude and presuming upon the favour of God? This depends entirely on how the word 'Christian' is understood. For some, the word has an ethnic connotation: all those born in a so-called 'Christian country' are Christians by birthright, unless they have subsequently chosen to remove themselves from this privilege.

Walking with God

For others, the word describes a certain way of living, not the lifestyle of an exceptional saint, but that of anyone who is reasonably kind and considerate: 'I'm as Christian as the next person.'

The New Testament definition of what it means to follow Christ naturally includes lifestyle, both in repentance and in active obedience, but what marks out the New Testament understanding from these other common usages of the term 'Christian' is a clear emphasis on the centrality of personal, saving faith. Jesus spelt it out to Nicodemus:

> *I tell you the truth, you cannot see the kingdom of God unless you are born again.*
>
> John 3:3

Peter emphasised the need for faith in Christ as the irreducible core of conversion:

> *Salvation is found in no-one else, for there is no other name under heaven given to men by which we must be saved.*
>
> Acts 4:12

Paul similarly stressed that faith in Christ is the source of our salvation:

> *If you confess with your mouth, 'Jesus is Lord,' and believe in your heart that God raised him from the dead, you will be saved.*
>
> Romans 10:9

Once we have put our trust in Christ, the New Testament consistently teaches that we are offered far more than forgiveness and a fresh start. To be sure, forgiveness for every stain of sin

70

is a remarkable gift of grace to the undeserving. But God goes further, by providing us with the righteousness of Christ. Paul spells out the implications:

> *God made him who had no sin to be sin for us, so that in him we might become the righteousness of God.*
>
> 2 Corinthians 5:21

> *Not having a righteousness of my own that comes from the law, but that which is through faith in Christ – the righteousness that comes from God and is by faith.*
>
> Philippians 3:9

Here is the glorious generosity of the atonement. Not only does the cross of Christ deal with our sin, but in the extravagant love of God we are freely and fully justified by faith. Our status before the Father is nothing less than the righteousness of Christ, for by faith in him we are indeed 'clothed with righteousness divine'. The cross of Christ does not merely deal with the past, it gives us confidence for the future. By faith in the crucified and risen Son of God, we are granted, in all its fullness, the right standing of Christ before the Father.

If we are to live confidently yet humbly in the service of Christ, a vital distinction must be drawn between our *status* in Christ and the *process* of becoming more like our Master. Where these two dimensions of Christian living are confused, perplexity is sure to follow, or even spiritual paralysis.

Becoming more like Christ in our character takes place in a quite different way to the immediate granting of the full status of citizenship of heaven. Paul speaks of being transformed by the Spirit 'with ever-increasing glory' (2 Cor. 3:18). To mature Christians he continues to give the advice to keep on taking off the old character and clothing themselves in the new

(Eph. 4:22–5; Col. 3:9–10,12). Speaking of himself, Paul stressed that he had not arrived at perfection, but 'forgetting what is behind and straining towards what is ahead, I press on towards the goal' (Phil. 3:13–14). This is the language not of status but of process: Christian character is the product of a lifetime of obedience and submission.

We can confuse the status and the process in several ways, all of which can cripple our effective Christian living. Jack accepted that once he had come to Christ he had received a new status before the Father, but he also assumed that he was now automatically beyond all possibility of sin. At first, his enthusiastic entry into new-found faith kept him going. A few weeks later, when selfishness reared its ugly head once again, Jack discovered that the total elimination of sin was less easy than he had thought. Then his confidence began to waver. If he had lost his sinlessness so easily, perhaps his salvation itself was equally fragile or even illusory.

Jenny fell into an equal but opposite confusion. She knew that character change was a slow and continuing process, but then she assumed that confidence in salvation was not possible until the mountain of character change had been ascended. If Jack lost his assurance of conversion because of one kind of confusion between the status and process of salvation, Jenny had never been able to enjoy any Christian confidence. All she could do was to try her best to work towards securing salvation at some uncertain future point in her life. Martin Luther described the agonies of uncertainty he experienced as a monk when he tried to work his passage to salvation in this way: 'However irreproachable my life as a monk, I felt myself in the presence of God to be a sinner with a most unquiet conscience, nor could I believe him to be appeased by the satisfaction I could offer.' Luther's relief when he discovered the New Testament's teaching on justification by faith was monumental, revolutionary and lifelong. Even though the journey into sanctification is yet to be completed, our God-given status through faith in Christ is already secure.

Pete's problem was different again. He knew that he was not perfect at the time of his salvation, and he was clear that he was saved not by his own works but by the cross of Christ. Two years later, Pete experienced a remarkable moment of submission to God, which he could only describe as 'absolute surrender'. As a result of this unforgettable encounter with God, Pete concluded that he had now entered sinless perfection. I remember clearly the moment he told me that it was at least ten days since he had last committed any kind of sin at all. When Pete once again rediscovered the reality of sin in his life, like Jack he was at risk of losing not only the false certainty of sinless perfection, but also the rightful privilege of a secure standing before the Father, justified through faith in the Son.

Charles Spurgeon once had breakfast with a man who claimed to have attained sinlessness. Accounts of the story vary as to whether a jug on the table was filled with milk or with water. Whatever the particular liquid, Spurgeon decided upon a practical test of the super-spiritual claim by depositing the contents of the jug over the man's head. This experiment in practical spirituality proved speedily conclusive, for it became immediately apparent that the man had not, after all, eradicated every last grain of sinfulness from his being ...

Today's Christians often have little appetite for the old technical words of Christian doctrine, but justification and sanctification are two vital principles, closely related and yet crucially distinct. We are saved (justification), we are being saved (sanctification), and we will be saved (glorification). We confuse justification and sanctification at our peril, with the result that either we begin to live in unreality, denying the continuing presence of the sinful nature, or alternatively we live without assurance, never having any confidence in the security and finality of our right standing before the Father.

Personal meditation

Pause for a moment of thankful prayer that you have received the 'righteousness that comes from God and is by faith' (Phil. 3:9).

2

The Inner Struggle

Just as we need to grasp the sharp distinction between the status and process of salvation, we need to understand clearly the ways in which the sinful nature continues to operate once we have come to faith. Nowhere in the New Testament is the interior struggle with selfishness more memorably expressed than in Romans 7, a chapter that inspired one of the great prayers in the English language, the General Confession:

> *I know that nothing good lives in me, that is, in my sinful nature. For I have the desire to do what is good, but I cannot carry it out. For what I do is not the good I want to do; no, the evil I do not want to do — this I keep on doing.*
>
> Romans 7:18–19

No one disputes the precisely observed intensity of this inner contradiction, which leads Paul to describe himself as a 'wretched man' (Rom. 7:24). There is, however, a great deal of debate concerning how to interpret the connection between the moral turmoil of Romans 7 and the spiritual victory of Romans 8. No fewer than ten interpretations have been offered in attempting to decide what stage of life Paul is portraying in this memorable description of conflicting aspirations and actions.

First, Paul is said to describe his lifelong experience as a practising Jew; second, his experience shortly before conversion, as he came under conviction of sin; third, his experience as an immature Christian, still struggling to put his new-found faith into practice. A second cluster of interpretations suggest that Paul is not so much describing his personal experience as dramatising the universal human condition: he is said to be describing, fourth, the condition of every Jew; fifth, all Jews who come under conviction of sin; sixth, all immature Christians. Others suggest that Paul is describing, seventh, the universal condition of all people, Jews and Gentiles alike, living in the consequences of the fall; or eighth, anyone coming under conviction of sin. Ninth, still others suggest that Paul is describing the experience of carnal Christians, struggling with sin ineptly and unsuccessfully in their own strength.

What all these interpretations have in common is the conviction that Romans 7 and 8 are to be interpreted sequentially. That is, at one stage of life, whether before or after conversion according to the various interpretations, we experience the inner contradictions of Romans 7. Subsequently, at least according to these schools of thought, we have the opportunity to graduate to the new level of existence in Romans 8, to the triumph of victorious living in the power of the Spirit of Christ.

There is, however, a quite different approach that does not hold before us the prospect, at least in this life, of making a permanent departure from Romans 7. This tenth interpretation proposes that, while Romans 7 certainly does describe the human condition at particular moments of personal and spiritual crisis, this does not exhaust its significance. With the precision and skill of a moral surgeon, Paul is performing the necessary task of exposing the cancer of sustained and instinctive sinfulness concealed within every human heart. Romans 7 is therefore a description of everyman and everywoman. The impact of

Christian conversion is not to remove the sinful nature, but rather to overthrow its tyranny. Far from ending, the struggle with the sinful nature is intensified after we come to faith. When we are born again, the inner fight has only just begun.

Augustine understood this conflict only too well in his own experience. When he wrote the *Confessions,* his remarkably precise and unflinchingly honest moral and spiritual self-examination, Augustine acknowledged and explored an unpleasant reality. The longer he served Christ, the more aware he became that a selfish undertow remained an integral part of his own existence. Sin was not a passing phase of immature Christian living, it was a daily and inescapable reality:

> *Heal me, in whose eyes I am now become a problem to myself. That is my infirmity.*

Augustine, *Confessions,* X:33

If we continue to live in Romans 7, not in constant defeat but as we endure a persistent inner struggle between goodness and selfishness, what is the relevance of Romans 8? The tenth interpretation explains that we live simultaneously in both chapters. From the perspective of our character and resources as fallen human beings, Romans 7 describes our condition precisely. However, from the perspective of new life in Christ, we have the additional resources of the Holy Spirit that are explored, indeed celebrated, in Romans 8.

Paul's teaching is more subtle than to invite us to decide which chapter describes more accurately our present moral and spiritual condition. He is better understood to propose that an adequate understanding of our potential as Christian believers and yet our continuing limitations as fallen sinners is only possible by developing a double or bi-polar perspective. According to this interpretation, which has been held by many Bible teachers including Augustine and Calvin, Spurgeon and Packer, at one and the same time every Christian lives simultaneously in both Romans 7 and 8. We know in our own experience both the triumph of grace and the sorrow of continuing sin. In Luther's phrase, the believer is *simul iustus et peccator*, at one and the same time justified and yet still a sinner. The sinful nature does indeed face the certain prospect of full and final eradication, but not this side of the grave.

This is why confession and repentance are an abiding reality for the Christian believer. We do not merely repent of sin once, upon our entry to saving faith. For all who continue to possess a sinful nature, repentance is not reduced to an introductory element of Christian initiation, nor merely a response to occasional lapses into sin; confession and repentance need to become a continuing and integral part of the spiritual life.

Self-evaluation

What do you think are the three most common pitfalls where the sinful nature still tends to get its way in your life?

3

Jesus and the Heart of Holiness

The very words 'confession' and 'holiness' carry for many an overload of negativity. Our concept of holy living has been gravely distorted, so that it seems to imply a way of life that is guaranteed to be cramped and narrow, parochial and predictable, safe and dull. Such 'holiness' seems to require an essentially legalistic and kill-joy approach to life, emphasising the many pleasures and indulgences that must always stay off-limits.

There are, of course, an irreducible number of restrictions on personal freedom that make life worth living. The fact that in Britain we are not allowed to drive at 100m.p.h. through the middle of a shopping centre while armed to the teeth with semi-automatic weapons can hardly be said to be a restriction on the individual that prevents personal fulfilment or the advancement of civilisation. The Ten Commandments provide a brilliant summary, succinct and yet profound, of the foundational laws on which a civilised society can be built. Holiness means living according to the Maker's instructions, which in turn means living life as it was intended: that is, life to the full. The removal of all restrictions would not amount to abundant life, but to a very hazardous form of anarchy.

The Pharisees took holy living very seriously. In their passionate concern to fulfil every detail of the law of Moses, they came to two conclusions. First, in order to keep the law, they decided to fence it, creating new boundaries, prohibiting many additional activities, in order to ensure that they protected themselves from trespassing on to any strictly forbidden territory. Second, fearing to fail in their practical obedience by neglecting the details of daily living, they extrapolated the implications of the law into the minutiae of life. As a result, absurd as it may seem, they not only tithed their money but even tithed their garden herbs!

Such extreme legalism seems almost laughable, but we have to recognise three implications. First, the intention of the Pharisees was originally good. They really wanted to embrace holy living. But the resultant lifestyle was a parody of God's positive holiness, living free from the damage that inevitably accompanies our indulgence of selfishness. While Jesus exemplifies life in all its abundance, the Pharisees exemplify a dark and dreary mutation, a false holiness, cramped within the bondage of legalism and negativity. Second, the approach of the Pharisees, however well intended, consistently failed to deliver the goods of true holiness. Jesus pinpointed the reality that all their outward religiosity was utterly impotent to shape or transform their inner life. He therefore laid against them the charge of hypocrisy:

> *You are like whitewashed tombs, which look beautiful on the outside but on the inside are full of dead men's bones and everything unclean.*

Matthew 23:27

The third implication of Pharisaism is the most uncomfortable, namely that the mutant holiness that they pursued did not die with them. Christians have similarly been guilty of excessive legalism and negativity, fencing the law and becoming pettily obsessed with the trivia of life. When the Church has sometimes drifted so far from Jesus' approach to holy living as to embrace the ways of his opponents, we have thereby put ourselves in jeopardy. It is often the Church that must now face Jesus' strictures against the Pharisees, including his charge of hypocrisy.

Jesus' summary of the law, quoting from the Old Testament, has a quite different emphasis:

> *One of them, an expert in the law, tested him with this question: 'Teacher, which is the greatest commandment in the Law?'*
>
> *Jesus replied: "Love the Lord your God with all your heart and with all your soul and with all your mind." This is the first and greatest commandment. And the second is like it: "Love your neighbour as yourself." All the Law and the Prophets hang on these two commandments.'*

Matthew 22:35–40

For Jesus, the central thrust of the law is to be found in love alone. The love that is expressed towards God must come from the totality of our being. In every dimension, every aspect of life, from our outward actions to the hidden recesses of our innermost being, Jesus calls us to a life devoted to expressing love towards the source of all love. With the second commandment, Jesus keeps to the same theme: we are not called to love others instead of loving ourselves, nor to love them despite an underlying distaste for ourselves. Rather, we are called to love ourselves within the love of God, and then to live in self-giving love, expressing towards others the same kind and measure of love with which we are learning to love ourselves.

When Jesus adds his new commandment to this summary of the law, his theme remains unchanged:

> *As I have loved you, so you must love one another.*
>
> John 13:34

Jesus' summary of the Old Testament law called us to self-giving love. But now he gives us a new benchmark for our love towards our fellow believers – no less than the measure of his own love for us. *Self-giving love* now extends to become *self-sacrificing love* in the imitation of the crucified Saviour. In a further strengthening of his own acute intensification of the love commands, Jesus also explains the connection between truly loving him and turning his teaching into action:

> *If any love me, they will obey my teaching.*
>
> John 14:23

Because Jesus consistently and constantly affirmed self-giving love as the focal point of holy living, his followers must always seek to do the same. Of course we continue to need to face up to wrong actions and thoughts that require confession and repentance, for the Ten Commandments have not expired. But Jesus takes us deeper into an understanding of holy living that expresses the very character of the living God. It is not enough to abstain from certain selfish indulgences. The measure of true holiness is whether we are learning to nurture a way of life that is shaped by self-giving love.

Paul spoke of God's love in terms of 'glorious grace, which he has freely given us in the One he loves ... the riches of God's grace that he lavished upon us' (Eph. 1:6–8). The supreme demonstration of God's love is the cross of Christ, where God gives up his own dear Son in order to provide redemption for a race who have consistently lived as God's enemies (Rom. 5:8). Such love is immeasurable in its extreme extravagance. Therefore, since the love of God is the perfect example towards which Christ beckons us, none have arrived and all are invited to continue a journey deeper into love. There is always more to discover of God's love for us, and more to discover of how to express that love both to one another and to a world of need.

Pause for thought

Is the love of Christ continuing to be your guiding light, or are there ways in which you could be drifting towards the attitudes of the Pharisees?

4

Dynamics of Confession

Since Christ calls us ever deeper into the love of God, there is a continuing need for confession of sin. While Satan seeks to condemn us, belabouring our inadequacies and failings, when the Holy Spirit convicts us of sin he points us always to the cross. Sin, forgiveness and a fresh start in the redemptive love of Christ, these three must always be combined in a truly biblical understanding of confession and repentance.

Paula's husband had left her, and she had drifted into seeking consolation in the arms of a colleague from work. She was looking for affection and comfort, but all she really achieved was a passing moment of casual sex. Afterwards she felt branded as a moral failure, even though no one else knew about their fleeting affair.

She knew that her actions were wrong, and she knew that Christ offered her forgiveness. But at heart level she became paralysed with guilt, unable to receive any experience of restoration in the love of Christ. As she spoke with my wife, Claire, and me, she eventually explained that she felt as if she had been branded across her forehead with a single word – 'Whore'. Others might drift casually through countless sexual liaisons, but Paula's one-night-stand left her estranged from Christ in a crushing sense of failure and self-recrimination.

Paula was in desperate need of help. Left to herself she could confess her sin to Christ, but never break through to a sense of forgiveness. As she confessed to us, she was extremely alert to every nuance of our reaction. If we had condemned her, any remaining glimmer of hope would have expired. If we had dismissed her wrongdoing casually, that would equally have left her stranded in her sin. She needed nothing less than Jesus' response to the woman caught in adultery, when he granted her forgiveness and yet called her to repentance:

> *Neither do I condemn you. Go now and leave your life of sin.*
> John 8:11

Paula needed to experience the forgiveness of Christ mediated to her through the response of her pastoral counsellors. Our reaction gave her hope, and from that moment her life began to be rebuilt. This should come as no surprise, since the letter of James contains the wise pastoral advice to confess our sins to one another (Jas. 5:16). To suggest that such confession should be made towards any and every Christian indiscriminately would be absurd. To propose public, compulsory confession of sin before the whole church would be tyrannous and cruel. Such excesses are beyond serious consideration. Most Protestants would also not want to adopt the Catholic practice of a regular, ritualised confession made always and only to a priest. However, in excluding the confessional, we must be careful not to swing to the opposite extreme of a totally individualistic approach to confessing sin, where Christ himself becomes our only Confessor. The pastoral reality is that, in many personal circumstances, confession to another Christian can provide the critical breakthrough from guilt and near despair, opening the doorway to a fresh encounter with the forgiving love of Christ.

In her twenties, Carla had a homosexual affair. It was a passing thing, at a time when her marriage was on the rocks. For the next twenty years she carried a sense of secret shame, telling no one of her profound sense of failing herself, her husband and her Lord. She was receiving counselling about an entirely different issue when an unexpected question was gently raised: 'Has there ever been anyone else?' This was really a word of knowledge, for the counsellor had suddenly received a very strong impression of a single word – 'adultery'.

In such circumstances it is crucial to be indirect: the counsellor could have mistaken a personal hunch for the prompting of the Holy Spirit. The indirect question, without reference to 'God telling me', left open the possibilities of either the counsellor being wrong or Carla choosing not to reveal her secret past. Carla began to weep quietly and said: 'No one has ever asked me that question before.' The truth was that Carla had been longing to confess the sin to someone, so that it could be dealt with, but had never known where to begin. However, in the first moments of confession, this oblique acknowledgment was the most she could bring herself to express.

A day or two later, the counsellor received a letter that set out the sad facts of the lesbian liaison. That was all that the counsellor needed to know and it would have been prurient even to consider exploring any details. Now the wall of silence had been broken, Carla had so much more to say to God. And so she wrote a second letter, this time not to her counsellor but to Christ, and sealed it in an envelope. At the next counselling session, the two of them prayed and then offered the unopened letter to Christ. The letter became a symbolic enactment of full repentance. The counsellor's task was not to read the letter, but to assist Carla, first in expressing her confession, and then in receiving forgiveness. The counsellor thanked God for the sacrifice of Christ, once for all, and for the decisive, atoning power of his shed blood, then a match was struck and the envelope was set alight. As the letter burned in the fireplace, a prayer of absolution was prayed. With tears of relief and joy, Carla's life was restored. She was no longer bound to the past with heavy chains of guilt, but was free to live in the present once again:

> *If anyone is in Christ, they are a new creation. The old has gone, the new has come!*
>
> 2 Corinthians 5:17

Mike sought prayer for healing because his life had become bound up in stress and anxiety. During counselling it became clear that these problems were merely symptoms of a deeper malaise. The root condition concerned past sin that Mike had never dealt with. I certainly do not wish to suggest that unconfessed sin is the universal root of stress, anxiety or sickness. Such a sweeping generalisation would be absurd. If everyone who was sick thought they needed to rummage around in their past to find an unconfessed sin sufficient to be considered the root cause of their present malaise, the result would be a church filled with anxious neurotics, constantly inventing past sins to explain present sickness. However, in rejecting such extremism, we must be careful not to exclude the possibility of a correlation between unconfessed sin and sickness in some individuals. When James set out his instructions for seeking prayer for healing, he did indicate the possibility of just such a connection:

> *Therefore confess your sins to each other and pray for each other so that you may be healed.*
>
> James 5:16

Praying for healing, expressing Christ's forgiveness, hearing a confession or praying over an unread letter that is then burned, these are just a few, practical ways in which we can assist one another. For every believer, there may be times when we need a supportive, pastorally sensitive fellow Christian to help us enter experientially into the living dynamic of confession and repentance, forgiveness and restoration. Confession is not about grovelling endlessly, wallowing in our sin, or being paralysed by past failure. Confession is the attitude with which we need to begin, but the place to which we can return every day is the cross of Christ. There we can enter once again into the liberating experience of forgiveness and a fresh start in the restoring love of the grace of God.

Personal response

Try writing a letter of confession and then, as you pray in repentance, burn it as a sign of your forgiveness in Christ, perhaps declaring the scriptural promise: 'The old has gone, the new has come!'

5

Recompense and Forgiveness

Confession is incomplete without repentance, and true repentance requires an act of will to change, with the Holy Spirit's help, the way in which we live. One often neglected aspect of repentant living is restitution. When Zaccheus experienced Jesus' offer of forgiveness and love, there was no need for anyone to explain to him the principle of restitution: he immediately declared a fourfold return of money to any he had cheated during his career as a tax collector. More than that, in recognition that the love of money was no longer the governing priority of his life, Zaccheus demonstrated practical repentance by announcing that he would also give away half of all his wealth to the poor (Luke 19:8–9). Neither Luke nor Jesus imply that wealth is intrinsically wrong or universally forbidden, but Zaccheus' encounter with Christ enabled him to be liberated from the tyranny of material acquisition as the ultimate goal of his life.

I remember vividly one elderly man telling me how repentance expressed in practical restitution became prominent in some towns during the Welsh Revival of 1904. Working men had for a long time considered railway property to be fair game for casual theft. When hundreds of local men came to Christ, they emptied their work-sheds of ill-gotten gains, restoring them to their rightful owner. So great was the quantity of stolen goods, that the railway had to open new buildings just to cope with the deluge. Now that's practical restitution!

Zaccheus' example is not an invitation to slavish legalism. No Christians need inflict upon themselves an exhaustive analysis of their entire lifetime, in search of every last moment of minuscule cheating that needs to be compensated. It is nothing less than absurd to imagine fifty- and sixty-year-old Christians sending a farthing to a sweet shop from which they stole a gobstopper as a child.

However, just as an over-insistence upon restitution can lead to abuse, there is an opposite danger of cheap grace, in which major instances of cheating are brushed hastily aside and conveniently forgotten. While avoiding petty excesses, we do well to examine ourselves for any instances of cheating that require proper recompense, without delay.

Repentance not only needs to find practical, outward expression, it must also take root in our inner life. Jesus plainly taught that our capacity to receive and experience the Father's forgiveness is critically dependent upon our willingness to forgive (Matt. 6:14–15). Some families cultivate a critical spirit from childhood years. By the time the children leave home, they have become grand masters of negativity, adept at destructive sarcasm or highlighting the weaknesses and deficiencies of others. Such an attitude can even masquerade as a rare and precious virtue: 'As a family, we set very high standards ... We don't suffer fools gladly.'

For others, the problem of an unforgiving spirit begins not with a general disposition but with a particular crisis. Once we choose to take offence and a grievance begins to be nursed, the results are predictable. Just as one rotten apple will corrupt a whole bowl of fruit if it is not removed quickly, one soured relationship can spread a creeping poison, so that we find it increasingly easy to become negative towards more and more people.

The trigger incident that provokes bitterness of heart can be traumatic or even, to the detached observer, apparently incidental. Rebekkah struggled with the bindweed of bitterness, constantly taking offence at the slightest thing. Through counselling, the trigger relationship for this attitude was unmasked. As a teenager, Rebekkah had been mocked by a teacher. Biting back the tears as she experienced the inner pain of ridicule, Rebekkah settled upon a life-shaping resolve: 'I will never, ever forgive this teacher.' Only when Rebekkah repented and chose to forgive could she be released from an instinctive, swiftly executed, vengeful attitude of heart that had made her, over the years, become unforgiving towards an ever-increasing number of people. What's more, just as Jesus warned, only when the teacher was forgiven could Rebekkah truly begin to experience the forgiveness of God.

We have recognised that bitterness has a tendency to spread, corrupting other relationships. Another dynamic of unforgiveness we need to grasp is that when we refuse to forgive, we become our own victims. Unforgiveness builds a bridge to the past over which the original hurt will travel to wound us again in the present. Nursing a grievance is like a child picking off a scab. The wound stays fresh. Only when we forgive the past can we begin to break free from its impact.

This may sound glib and insensitive to those who have suffered extreme hurt. While some may be able to express forgiveness as an act of will when they recognise the wisdom of Jesus' teaching, others are likely to need the assistance of pastoral counselling and should not feel a burden of additional guilt because they are unable to break through instantaneously to a forgiving spirit. Forgiveness is the destination we must choose to seek as followers of Christ, but for some the journey will be slow and painful, best travelled in the supportive company of an understanding counsellor or friend.

Sometimes bitterness takes root because of a hard time faced by our partner or children. Mary spoke with me about how Frank, her husband, had been badly treated by a church some ten years before. After such an interval it seemed to me relatively unimportant to attempt to unravel whether Mary and her husband had been more sinned against than sinning. I therefore asked what I took to be the most important question: 'Have you forgiven them?'

'Yes,' Mary replied, 'I have forgiven them completely.' As she spoke the words she knew I wanted to hear, Mary's body language told a different story. One hand closed into a fist and began to pummel the other hand vigorously. Mary was not conscious of what her hands were doing, but their eloquent mime unmasked the secrets of her heart. 'If they were here,' her hands said, 'I would like to show them just how much wrong they did.' It is relatively easy for many of us to control our words and even our tone of voice. Through body language the secrets of our inner life leak out from under the veneer of repression and respectable Christian behaviour.

Mary's self-entrapment reveals a further dynamic of bitterness. At the time of their difficulties, Frank had been exemplary, constantly and genuinely forgiving others. This exasperated Mary all the more. 'If he won't stand up for himself,' she resolved, 'I'll have to do it for him.' Nursing a grievance on her husband's behalf, Mary felt thoroughly vindicated in her unforgiveness. It was, in her eyes, a conclusive demonstration of her devotion to her husband that she had cultivated a bitterness she was determined never to relinquish. Only by choosing to forgive others could Mary break free from the past. She would know little of God's present forgiveness until past grievance was released.

Husbands and wives, parents and children, close friends and colleagues, we need to make sure we never cultivate an unforgiving spirit on behalf of those closest to us. No matter how justifiable such an attitude might appear, it is ultimately self-destructive and utterly alien to Jesus' way of living, for he was always generous in forgiveness and self-giving love. Those who walk in unforgiveness are self-condemned to know in their own lives little of the forgiveness of God.

Personal evaluation

Is there any nursed grievance, harboured grudge or root of bitterness in your life? How will you make sure that it is evicted without delay?

6

Confident in Grace

Without the cross, confession would still be necessary, but we could obtain no real confidence that we were truly saved. Meditating upon the cross is immeasurably enriching to our praying, for it is the decisive, historical event which opened new opportunities, a new destiny for the human race. The cross is the pivot of history, the ultimate demonstration and redemptive action of the self-giving love of God.

Isaac Watts' most famous hymn speaks about surveying 'the wondrous cross'. This can take place at three distinct levels. First, there is an *intellectual survey*, a thoughtful consideration of the doctrinal significance of God's self-substitution on behalf of a rebellious race. Second, there is an *imaginative survey*, entering into the dramatic intensity of the historical events. Third, there is an *existential survey*, in which we recognise our responsibility and benefit from Christ's sacrifice, and make our own response of willing surrender. All three dimensions of meditation on the cross can be found in Watts' 'When I survey', and all three are inexhaustible. The more we meditate upon the cross, the more we recognise the riches of grace that are ours in Christ.

In reaction against traditional Catholic veneration of a crucifix, many Protestant Christians have tended to prefer the symbol of an empty cross. This avoids the possibility of substituting worship of the artefact for worship of Christ himself. It affirms that the work of the cross is ultimately incomplete without the triumph of the resurrection. It also emphasises that Christ's sacrifice is once for all: no further sacrifice will ever be necessary to supplement the atoning death of the Saviour. There is, however, a danger that Protestant Christians may rush too fast from Good Friday to Easter Sunday, not pausing long enough to dwell on the darkness, trauma and suffering that marked those hours from when the nails first split Christ's skin until his body was laid to rest in the garden tomb.

Throughout the centuries, many believers have found it rewarding to meditate upon a painting of the cross. Much Byzantine art portrays a crucified Christ characterised by absolute serenity, the Lord of the cosmos in consummate control, even as he begins to taste death. Medieval European art often emphasised the stark reality of his suffering, depicting a Christ racked with torturous pain, his body twisted and writhing. Such paintings take us beyond a conceptual, detached approach to the crucifixion, bringing into focus the double drama of Christ's death as victim and yet conqueror.

Meditating upon the cross can be enriched by constructing a crown of thorns, or obtaining a crude iron nail similar to those used at Roman executions. The stark symbols of the crucifixion can then be kept before the eyes for focused and prolonged meditation. For more delicate sensibilities, such severe aids to meditative prayer are too harsh, too distressing. Others will be broken out of coolness, complacency or a casual attitude to the cross of Christ, by an 'in-your-face' confrontation with the pain-stricken, brute realities of death by crucifixion.

Such meditation is certainly not perverse or self-indulgent, let alone sadistic. The more we grasp the costly realities of the cross, the more we can enter into its benefits. Christ as he hung there was indeed 'made sin for us', and just as certainly, by faith in him, we have become 'the righteousness of God' (2 Cor. 5:21). For every moment of prayer dwelling upon our inner depths of sin, we do well to spend at least as much time considering the immensity of God's redemptive love, etched in the crucified agonies of our Saviour.

Communion, the great love feast of the Church, was given to us by Christ to express our profound dependence upon the sacrificial Lamb of God. The tokens of his body and blood speak of our need to feed upon Christ in humble surrender. The fact that bread and wine were the staple diet of Middle Eastern peasants speaks of the sacrifice being paid for all, irrespective of background, for the love of Christ and the redemptive power of his cross are not locked up within some exotic, rarefied banquet of the privileged few. The unadorned simplicity of this meal also speaks of everyday living. Not only in an 'official' communion service at church, but every time bread and wine pass our lips, we can eat and drink in remembrance of Christ's cross, in participation in his body and blood, and in expectation of his glorious return.

Personal meditation

Take some time to reflect upon the enormous import and sacrifice of the cross, the pivot of human history. You may like to assist your meditation with a painting of the crucifixion, some music, a crown of thorns, a nail, or simply some bread and wine.

7

Bible Meditation

THE ARREST, TRIAL, CRUCIFIXION AND BURIAL
– LUKE 22:47–23:56

We can become overfamiliar with the Easter story, losing sight of the extraordinary intensity of these epoch-changing events as we rush to the triumph of the resurrection. Read Luke's narrative slowly, preferably two or three times, remembering that those who were a part of this history, apart from Christ himself, had no concept of the resurrection that was to follow. For Jesus' followers, these events seemed at first to be a bewildering disaster and an unmitigated tragedy.

Enter into the events from the contrasting perspectives of several eyewitnesses, for example:

Through the eyes of Peter

The disciples' spokesperson became the great betrayer, denying his Master three times, even as Jesus had prophesied. Then Peter rushed out into the night, weeping bitterly in solitary despair. He had lost his dream of a triumph in Jerusalem, with Jesus expelling the Roman occupying army by Messianic force. Peter had also lost all self-belief, as he sank from vigorous leadership into the evasive and slippery denials of a coward.

Through the eyes of the crowd

They had welcomed Jesus to the city with palm branches, but soon they bayed for his death. As he hung on the cross, they sneered at the apparent impotence faced with his own death of the man whose healing power so many had once sought.

Through the eyes of Pilate

At first he sympathised with Jesus, finding no basis for a charge, but Pilate lacked the moral fibre to stand up for the innocent when the crowd demanded that Jesus be crucified.

Through the eyes of the soldiers

They may have expected trouble when they came to arrest Jesus, but soon took callous pleasure in mocking and abusing him.

Through the eyes of the criminals

One hurled insults, scornfully demanding that Jesus save all three from crucifixion. The other offered a humble prayer, recognising that Jesus alone was facing an undeserved execution.

Through the eyes of the women

Though Peter denied Jesus, and others fled from the soldiers, the women maintained their faithful and courageous vigil throughout his last hours. No sense of personal danger could stand in the way of their devotion to Jesus, to his very last breath. Helpless and deeply sorrowful, they stayed near the cross to the bitter end.

Through the eyes of Joseph of Arimathea

A member of the Council, Joseph had been helpless to protect Jesus from death, even though he had not consented to the judgment. He risked his own life by asking Pilate for the body, then laid it to rest in an unused garden tomb, that had presumably been hewn from the rock for Joseph or one of his family. Now it became what Joseph supposed to be his last expression of devotion to the man he had admired from afar.

Through the eyes of the centurion

Crucifixion was a part of a centurion's profession as a career soldier. He had seen men face the agonies of death in many ways: brave and stubborn silence, agonised screams, pathetic appeals for last-minute reprieval, or the fearful rage of those whose final energies were directed in burning anger against their executioners. Never had he seen a man die in the manner of Jesus, and so the world-weary professional soldier expressed his astonished conviction: 'Surely this man was the Son of God!' (Mark 15:39).

Through the eyes of Jesus

As he embraces the appalling reality of death by crucifixion, Jesus offers not one word of self-vindication. His only prayer for his murderers is an appeal for divine forgiveness.

Poems, Prayers and Hymns for Reflection

THE AGONY
Philosophers have measured mountains,
Fathomed the depths of seas, of states, and kings,
Walk'd with a staff to heaven, and traced fountains:
But there are two vast, spacious things,
The which to measure it doth more behove:
Yet few there are that sound them; Sin and Love.

Who would know Sin, let him repair
Unto Mount Olivet; there shall he see
A man so wrung with pains, that all his hair,
His skin, his garments bloody be.
Sin is that press and vice, which forceth pain
To hunt his cruel food through every vein.

Who know not Love, let him assay
And taste that juice, which on the cross a pike
Did set again abroach; then let him say
If ever he did taste the like.
Love is that liquor sweet and most divine,
Which my God feels as blood; but I, as wine.

George Herbert, 1593–1633

From GOOD FRIDAY, 1613. RIDING WESTWARD
O Saviour, as Thou hang'st upon the tree;
I turn my back to thee, but to receive
Corrections, till thy mercies bid thee leave.
O think me worth thine anger, punish me,
Burn off my rusts, and my deformity,
Restore thine image, so much, by thy grace,
That thou may'st know me, and I'll turn my face.
John Donne, 1573–1631

THE JESUS PRAYER

Since we are sinful by nature, an extremely valuable type of prayer is a general confession, a non-specific expression of both our condition of heart and our profound, continuing dependence on the grace of God. Many have found an ancient prayer of the Eastern Orthodox Church to be enormously helpful in expressing this kind of confession:

> *Lord Jesus Christ, Son of God,*
> *Have mercy on me, a sinner.*

The traditional way to benefit from this prayer is by slow and methodical repetition. Those who think that Jesus' prohibition of idle repetition stands against all manner of repetitive prayer will be unable to benefit from this prayer to the full. This is not a misguided attempt to bludgeon a reluctant God into answering prayer by remorseless repetition. Nor is it a repetition born of anxiety, repeating a desperate request for forgiveness in the forlorn hope that one day it might actually be granted. Rather, this prayer invites repetition as a way of centring our mind and heart upon the pivotal truths of human existence. Just as someone tuning a guitar will repeatedly strike the strings, bringing them to the correct pitch, and will then continue to test them from time to time, to ensure that the pitch is held, the repetition of this prayer is about retuning ourselves towards a right relationship with the living God.

The prayer is in two movements. The first is an affirmation of the essential identity of Jesus Christ. It recalls the ancient Christian acrostic which was marked by the sign of the fish. *Ichthus*, the Greek word for 'fish', was understood by the early Christians to summarise several essential saving truths: Jesus Christ, Son of God, Saviour.

Having declared the eternal identity of Christ, the second line of the Jesus Prayer defines the human condition in relation to the Son of God. We are sinners, without exception, in need of the mercy that our Saviour alone can provide. The second line, therefore, acknowledges not only our sinfulness but also our absolute dependence on the grace of God, made available to us through the atoning sacrifice of the Son. In eloquent simplicity, the prayer expresses humility and faith in equal measure.

As the prayer is repeated, it should not be rushed through in thoughtless repetition, like some idle mantra. This succinct summary of gospel truth needs to be repeated slowly, savouring each phrase, taking time to focus on the perfectly balanced truths of the person of Christ and the forgiveness he brings to sinners. Some find the prayer is helpfully expressed while walking, dwelling upon each line for the duration of two paces. Others find the prayer a profitable discipline at moments of enforced inactivity, waiting for a bus or train, in a traffic jam or a supermarket checkout queue.

Another way of pacing the prayer is to connect its two phrases with slow and regular breathing. A suggestive connection between praying and breathing is found in the languages of the Bible, for the Hebrew and Greek words for Spirit share the same literal meaning, that is 'breath'. As we pray in time with our breathing, we seek the inspiring touch of the breath of God. Care must of course be taken to avoid any risk of hyperventilation, and so our breathing should be kept regular, relaxed and measured.

Here is a practical exercise in praying the Jesus Prayer. As you breathe in, silently pray the first line. Symbolically, as you inhale the oxygen that is life-giving to our bodies, you seek to inhale the truth of the person of Christ, who is life-giving to our spirits. As you breathe out, you silently pray the second line. Just as you exhale the carbon dioxide that is poisonous to our physical well-being, you seek to give over to Christ the sin that is destructive of our spiritual well-being. Repeating the Jesus Prayer in this way, accompanied by slow, relaxed, deep breathing, can be enormously enriching, centring our meditation upon the glorious riches of Christ made available to each one of us personally through his death in our place. Just as a gourmet savours delicious food or a fine wine, this is a prayer to be dwelt upon at leisure. It takes time for these glorious truths to shape the mind and enrich the spirit as we learn to drink deeply of the grace of Christ.

My song is love unknown,
My Saviour's love to me;
Love to the loveless shown,
That they might lovely be.
O who am I,
That for my sake
My Lord should take
Frail flesh, and die?

He came from his blest throne
Salvation to bestow;
But men made strange, and none
The longed-for Christ would know:
But O! My Friend,
My Friend indeed,
Who at my need
His life did spend.

Sometime they strew his way,
And his sweet praises sing;
Resounding all the day
Hosannas to their King:
Then 'Crucify!'
Is all their breath,
And for his death
They thirst and cry.

They rise and needs will have
My dear Lord made away;
A murderer they save,
The Prince of life they slay;
Yet cheerful he
To suff'ring goes,
That he his foes
From thence might free.

In life, no house, no home
My Lord on earth might have;
In death, no friendly tomb,
But what a stranger gave.

What may I say?
Heaven was his home;
But mine the tomb
Wherein he lay.

Here might I stay and sing,
No story so divine;
Never was love, dear King!
Never was grief like Thine.
This is my Friend,
In whose sweet praise
I all my days
Could gladly spend.
Samuel Crossman, 1624–83

Alas! And did my Saviour bleed?
And did my Sovereign die?
Would he devote that sacred head
For such a worm as I?

Was it for sins that I had done
He groaned upon the tree?
Amazing pity! Grace unknown!
And love beyond degree!

Well might the sun in darkness hide,
And shut his glories in,
When Christ, the mighty Maker, died
For man the creature's sin.

Thus might I hide my blushing face
While his dear cross appears,
Dissolve my heart in thankfulness,
And melt mine eyes to tears.

But drops of grief can ne'er repay
The debt of love I owe:
Here, Lord, I give myself away:
'Tis all that I can do.
Isaac Watts, 1674–1748

A hymn by Charles Wesley

Millions the Christian name
Without the cross receive,
Servants of men and slaves of fame
In ease and pleasures live;
Following the world his foe
They throng the spacious road,
Nor will in Jesu's footsteps go
By Calvary to God.

But better taught by grace
His doctrines I approve,
Cheerful his daily cross embrace,
And all his sufferings love:
With joy I follow him
Who once for sinners died,
And nothing know, desire, esteem
But Jesus crucified.

CHAPTER IV

TO GOD WITH LOVE

Praying for others

What various hindrances we meet
    In coming to the mercy-seat!
Yet who, that knows the worth of prayer,
    But wishes to be often there!

Prayer makes the darkened cloud withdraw,
    Prayer climbs the ladder Jacob saw,
    Gives exercise to faith and love,
    Brings every blessing from above.

Restraining prayer, we cease to fight;
Prayer makes the Christian's armour bright;
    And Satan trembles when he sees
    The weakest saint upon his knees.

While Moses stood with arms spread wide,
    Success was found on Israel's side;
But when, through weariness, they failed,
    That moment Amalek prevailed.

Have you no words, ah! Think again!
Words flow apace when you complain
    And fill your fellow creature's ear
    With the sad tale of all your care.

Were half the breath thus vainly spent
    To heaven in supplication sent,
Your cheerful song would oftener be,
'Hear what the Lord has done for me.'

                                    William Cowper

1

The Mystery of Intercession

No one has ever been able to fathom how intercessory prayer really works. It is an enigma enfolded in mysteries. From the perspective of divine sovereignty, if everything is pre-ordained prayer would seem essentially futile, a mere mouthing of pious hopes with no possibility of fulfilment. Unless, of course, the act of prayer itself is pre-ordained, in which case the prayer's fulfilment is guaranteed. In such a world, prayer would have some nominal kind of meaning, echoing the predetermined purposes of God, but life itself would not, stripped of every last fragment of freedom and dignity, for we would be mere automatons, robotically intoning prayer requests we had been programmed to utter at that particular moment.

At the same time, our experience of unanswered prayers would also have to be completely predetermined, adding a further dimension of futility to both prayer and human existence. In short, if every last, minuscule detail of life was settled in advance, our intercessory prayers would have little or no meaning. Nor would any personal resolve to pray ardently or not to bother with prayer, for that too would have been sovereignly disposed. In such a world, like pre-programmed factory robots we would each fulfil our allotted and empty task, without meaning or value.

From a quite different perspective, some consider our prayers to be the absolutely crucial spur which causes God to act on our behalf. Some see this in terms of spiritual warfare: the mountain of prayer must be built to overcome the resistance or tyranny of evil. Just as overstating the sovereignty of God in terms of the absolute divine predetermining of life's every last detail strips prayer of meaning, overstating our contribution to spiritual warfare strips God of either his power or his love. If our prayers are needed to overcome evil before God can act, then God is less than almighty. It is no longer Christ who is the Victor, through his death and resurrection, but rather the Church that is the mighty conqueror, as we overcome the power of evil through our prayers, and so open the way for God to work in love.

If our prayers are needed to provoke an all-powerful God into action, a very considerable problem arises with the quality of divine love. In this model of prayer, God is by no means unable to act on our behalf, but he does appear to be unwilling, detached and indifferent to our concerns and circumstances unless goaded into action by sufficient prayer. If prayer alone could overcome evil or stir an indifferent God into action, the weight of human responsibility in prayer would swiftly become intolerable. The simple conclusion would have to be drawn that any experience of evil, suffering or anything less than the triumphant advance of the Church was directly and completely our responsibility. In such a world, no one would ever dare to cease from prayer. Any Christians who genuinely hold such an extreme view will soon be overwhelmed by a catastrophic and infinite sense of personal failure to pray the triumph of good into being. This approach produces Christians who are not robotic, but neurotic.

Still others suggest that the great problem with prayer is not the mechanism by which it brings results, but the fact that not all prayers are answered positively. My own conviction is that nothing could be more horrendous than a world where prayer automatically secured instant divine action. Imagine the devastating impact on election night if God guaranteed to fulfil every prayer request. Before the results begin to come in, opinion polls indicate a huge swing to the left. The first Christian to pray is a right-winger: 'Please don't let the left in!' Immediately the TV stations report a new swing to the right, blaming their computers for this sudden reversal in their predictions. Faced with this news, a left-winger prays a cry of passion: 'I would rather have the country led by a dog than by the leader of the right of centre party.' A sudden news flash appears on TV screens across the nation, explaining that the right has a new and unexpected leader with unmistakably canine features ...

If I was guaranteed 100 per cent success rate in answered prayer, I would never dare to pray again. The responsibility would be too great, the risks too high. As a teenager I would have married several girls before I even met my wife, as a result of a fleeting moment of besotted infatuation – 'O Lord, may she be the one for me!' My judgment is too fallible, my perspective too limited. In such a world, the very act of prayer would bring an intolerable level of responsibility.

Somewhere between these extremes lies reality. Our prayers are neither pointless nor all-powerful. A 'success rate' of 100 per cent is never going to be achieved, no matter how hard we may try. Such realism is not a reason to give up on prayer, but rather to continue with the mysterious privilege of partnership with God. We may not understand quite how prayer works, but we do enjoy both scriptural and evidential encouragement to persist in prayer. Scriptural, because there we find repeated encouragement to engage in this task. Evidential, because we have discovered the simple reality that prayer works: when we pray, we see the love of God in action. This is how we can continue to live with the double mystery of answered and unanswered prayer. As an Anglican archbishop once observed: when we persist in prayer, positive 'coincidences' have a tendency to multiply.

Personal evaluation

Spend a few moments recalling some of the 'coincidences' that have arisen when you have prayed for others. Give thanks to God for the mysterious privilege of intercessory prayer.

2

Motivated by Love

If we don't pray because results are guaranteed, and we don't pray because we fully understand the dynamics of how prayer works, why do we pray for others at all? The primary motivation behind intercessory prayer is undoubtedly love. When we feel for the needs of others, we instinctively turn that compassion into prayer. For the Christian there is simply no choice: inasmuch as we love, we are bound to pray.

Our reasons for prayer are instinctive, evidential and scriptural. Instinctive, because prayer is the natural consequence of love. Evidential, because we see the benefits of intercession. Scriptural, because the Bible encourages us to intercede:

> *Do not be anxious about anything, but in everything, by prayer and petition, with thanksgiving, present your requests to God.*

> Philippians 4:6

Paul's words are chosen carefully. He is hardly suggesting that intercessory prayer leads to an easy life, since he is writing under house arrest, facing the possibility of imminent state execution. What Paul does is to show us how to set life's pressures in a creative context, viewing them from the perspective of God's loving attentiveness to his children. All things, the apostle explains, can be brought before God, who is never indifferent to our circumstances and feelings. The kind of praying that Paul commends has two distinctive qualities. First, our petitions need to be accompanied by *thanksgiving*: the urgency of a particular need should never be allowed to obliterate God's intrinsic praiseworthiness and the discipline of expressing due thankfulness, even in times of personal adversity. Second, our needs should be presented before God as *requests*. This recalls the ancient tradition of commoners presenting a petition to the king. The request is an appeal for effective and merciful action, presented by one who has no right to make any demands upon their Lord.

Jesus' parable of the importunate widow certainly encourages us to persist in prayer and not lose heart easily (Luke 18:1–8), but our praying should always remain strictly free from any hectoring, insistent or demanding tone. We come not to pester, cajole or provoke our God into action, but merely to present our requests with humility. We plead for divine action in the way we think best, but we submit to divine wisdom, always acknowledging there may be a greater good, a better way, that we are unable to discern or determine. Faced with even the most severe storms of life, the way of trusting petition and patient thanksgiving secures for us a hiding place in God.

Just as we pray for others because we love them, we pray to the God whom we love. Augustine once summed up holy living in the phrase, 'Love God and do what you like.' By this he meant that lifestyle grows out of relationship: the more we love God, the more we will choose to please him in the way we live. In a similar way we can sum up intercession: 'Love Christ, and pray what you like.' This is the natural implication of Jesus' promise: 'Then the Father will give you anything you ask in my name' (John 15:16). Jesus is hardly suggesting that we use his name as a kind of magical formula, as if attaching it to any request, however arbitrary, wilful or foolish, is a guarantee of automatic results. The more we love Jesus, the more we conform to his ways and submit to his Lordship, the more wisely and effectively we shall pray. Requests born of wise and submissive love are the only kind of 'anything you ask' prayers that Jesus has promised the Father will fulfil.

Some try to reduce effective intercession to a technique. If only the right phrases can be used, at the right time of day, in the company of the right people. If only sin is confessed deeply enough, Satan bound strongly enough, our request uttered boldly enough, the divine answer will be delivered by return of post. The New Testament offers an entirely different perspective, for love and faith are the only essential ingredients of Christian intercession. We present requests for those we love before the God of love, whom we seek to love with all our heart.

Practical response

Tell God about your love for some who are close to you. Identify the qualities within them that you admire the most. What is the best request that you can make for them?

3

Letting People Know

It is a curious custom of church life that the people who disapprove of a leader are far more inclined to let it be known than the people who are encouraging and supportive. Some leaders have told me that it was not until their leaving party that they discovered how many people in the church had really appreciated their ministry. How we need to break free from such reticence! When the writer to the Hebrews instructs us to 'Encourage one another daily, as long as it is called "Today"' (Heb. 3:13), this clearly means that not a single day should ever pass without our seeking to provide encouragement to another believer. Sometimes when I take a church weekend I make a practical suggestion for the coming week, inviting everyone to send at least one card of encouragement and appreciation to someone in their church whose ministry they have tended to take for granted.

Just as we are often reticent in expressing encouragement, many of us instinctively keep to ourselves the fact that we are praying for others. The apostle Paul had a quite different approach: he not only prayed for people, he positively relished the opportunity to tell them about his prayers:

In all my prayers for all of you, I always pray with joy...
                                                    Philippians 1:4

And this is my prayer: that your love may abound more and more...

Philippians 1:9

I pray that you, being rooted and established in love, may have power, together with all the saints, to grasp how wide and long and high and deep is the love of Christ, and to know this love that surpasses knowledge – that you may be filled to the measure of all the fulness of God.

Ephesians 3:17–19

Similarly, Paul is not averse to presenting others with a very specific prayer request:

Pray for us too, that God may open a door for our message, so that we may proclaim the mystery of Christ, for which I am in chains. Pray that I may proclaim it clearly, as I should.

Colossians 4:3–4

Here we should note the focus of Paul's intercession, which is the advance of the gospel rather than his personal comfort. His concern is not that the Colossians should major on praying for an improvement in his circumstances, that is, his release from prison. Nor does he ask them to conduct extensive and exhaustive 'spiritual warfare' on his behalf, in order to repel the principalities and powers who have constrained the progress of his apostolic witness. Paul's abiding concern is not that he might enjoy an easy life or public acclaim for his Christian convictions. Rather, he wants to be an overcomer in all circumstances, turning evil to good, demonstrating the resurrection hope even in the most difficult circumstances. Therefore, when in chains, rather than simply praying for his release, he prays for the fulfilment of his primary objective: to be an effective witness for Jesus Christ.

This overcoming capacity is summed up in the way Paul describes himself. The chains around his arms demonstrate that he is a captive of the Roman authorities, but with the eyes of faith Paul sees himself as one under a higher jurisdiction. Christ is the cause of his captivity: 'I am in chains for Christ' (Phil. 1:13), and Christ is also his ultimate captor: 'Paul, a prisoner of Christ Jesus' (Philem. 1). While the Romans can chain him or even kill him, it is Christ alone who has settled his life's purpose and his eternal destiny. Therefore the honour of Christ and the advance of his kingdom are pivotal to Paul's requests for prayer.

Practical response

Is there someone you can encourage, either by expressing your appreciation or by telling them that you are praying for them?

4

Releasing Requests

Just as the mystery of intercession can put off some Christians from ever bringing requests before the Father's throne, others reduce the vast panoply of prayer to this one aspect. When I was converted, as a teenager, we received much encouragement to intercede but little or no teaching or help with many other dimensions of prayer, such as biblical meditation, contemplation and receiving God's love.

The customary aid to prayer in evangelical circles in those days was the prayer list. Everyone had a list, to which new themes were added as you discovered more individuals or nations for whom to pray. The extra-devout were also said to keep a second list, a record of answered prayers, ideally with dates attached. I remember vividly one film in which a devout Christian leader showed us his prayer diary, requests and answers precisely tabulated. It seemed that effective intercessory prayer required nothing less than the meticulously organised tabulatory skills of double-entry book-keeping.

In youthful enthusiasm I quickly encountered two problems with this method. First, I could never find the time to tabulate requests and answers in such a schematic way. Second, I found it relatively easy to add new names to my prayer list, but very difficult to remove any. If I had not kept in touch with someone's circumstances, did this entitle me to strike them off the list, or should I repent of such indifference and redouble my efforts in prayer on their behalf? The result was predictable, and I suspect that many others have faced the same impasse. As the prayer list grew ever longer, the catalogue of requests became ever more cursory. Praying began to feel like a long-distance race in which every lap of the track became longer than the previous lap. Other dimensions of prayer could hardly be explored, since there was little enough time to stumble through the ever-expanding list of people and needs. Eventually exhaustion was bound to set in, until at last the mountainous prayer list was abandoned, leaving behind a residual guilt that perhaps I should have continued praying for those people just a little longer.

Despite these unpleasant forays into unreality, I do not entirely disapprove of prayer lists. I think all of us benefit from a sense of focus in prayer, knowing for whom we have accepted a particular responsibility to pray. Some may pray for their family and church leaders, others may pray for their home group or several missionaries, or even work their way through a church directory. Used wisely, a prayer list can be a useful aid in the discipline of prayer. But we do need to protect the naive and enthusiastic from an over-ambitious endeavour to pray regularly for every single person they encounter. As I travel around preaching, it is inevitable that many people will ask me to pray for their personal and family needs, their church or their nation. I have made a habit of never promising to continue to pray for them. Instead I pray there and then, discharging the responsibility of Christian love while remaining free from the tyranny of an ever-expanding prayer list.

I have some rampant climbing plants in my garden. If they are kept in check, they provide a vigorous and decorous covering for a fence and pergola. Allowed to run riot, they would soon overpower the more delicate plants, reducing order, beauty and harmony to a tangled chaos, quickly turning my garden into a suburban jungle. Prayer lists can be similarly disposed to rampant growth: if you find using one helpful, be sure to keep it in check!

Practical response

If you have never kept a prayer list, is there anyone you would like to begin to pray for regularly? If you have been keeping a prayer list, but it has run out of control, is it time for a radical and ruthless pruning?

5

Praying with Others

My teenage attendance at church prayer meetings was not encouraging. Most people had obviously chosen to take the night off. Those who attended were the committed core of the church, but their undoubted commitment was not matched with a sense of adventure or eagerness in prayer. The phrase that best sums up this lamentable experience is *well-intentioned but boring*.

Praying together requires effort, imagination and creativity. Above all, for people to feel that a prayer meeting is a worthwhile use of time, we need to bring our requests in an environment of faith. This is why prayer and praise work well together. Praise establishes a context in which to ask for God to act. In addition to songs of worship, it is good to provide opportunities for personal testimony so that we can hear first-hand reports of the love of God in action, together with feedback on answered prayers from previous meetings.

Songs, testimonies and prayers of praise all need to be kept fresh. If the same routine is repeated at every prayer meeting, with the same themes and the same people praying, the dynamic reality of serving a God who reaches out in love will be lost. In its place we begin to sink back into a ritual that becomes increasingly predictable and empty.

One simple stimulus is to stand together for open prayer. A change of posture may seem a small step, but it is surprising how big a difference it can make to the mood of a meeting and to the willingness of people to really enter into a time of praise. Prayer requests are voiced with greater faith and expectancy in an environment of praise. Here we must acknowledge two contrasting dangers. On the one hand, we can pray together without faith, going through the motions of voicing our requests with no real expectation that anything will happen as a result. The history of superficial praying began early, for this was how the church prayed in Acts 12, when they could not believe that their prayers had been answered so fast and the liberated Peter really was standing outside the door.

The second great danger is to pray not with too little faith, but with too much naive optimism. Authentic prayer with faith is very different from the mere expression of wish-fulfilment fantasies. High-octane exuberance may excite us to ask for the earth, but the mere froth of superficial excitement soon passes. Without a disciplined focus on Christ, his cross and resurrection, Christians have a tendency to swing between the unreality of gullible triumphalism and the equal and opposite unreality of cynical disillusionment, from asking for the clouds to asking for nothing at all. We need to learn how to walk that creative and inclusive path of faith mapped out by the apostle Paul, when he spoke of his double aspiration in following Christ: to know the power of his resurrection *and* the fellowship of sharing in his sufferings (Phil. 3:10).

If our praying together requires a positive environment of genuine faith, there also needs to be room to accept and embrace the darker side of life: the place of struggle, uncertainty and disappointment. The pastoral justification for including life's strains in our prayer meetings is the simple reality that sooner or later everyone will pass through this kind of phase of life: we not only want to provide support for those who are presently walking through pain, but we also have the opportunity to demonstrate to those in easier circumstances that Christian faith and hope are equally relevant and real in even the bleakest seasons of life.

We can approach with confidence the task of including the darker side of life because of the remarkable precedent found in the psalms of lament. Ancient Hebrew poets were not afraid to express their sorrows and frustrations before their Lord.

> *Hear me, O God, as I voice my complaint;*
> *protect my life from the threat of the enemy.*
> Psalm 64:1

The compilers of the Psalter, the hymn book of ancient Israel, were not disposed to establish a collection that sang only of triumph and joy, always looking on the bright side of life. They had the wisdom to provide songs for life's every season. Those walking through sorrow, just as much as those enjoying much happiness, can find psalms that express with great eloquence and precision the deepest feelings of their inner life. Today, many are tempted to swing from one extreme to another, from denial, repressing the shadowed side of life, to despair, in which the darkness seems to have enfolded us. A far more profound spiritual discipline is found within the psalms of lament (for example, Psalms 6, 38, 88, 102, 130, 142). First there is the release of being able to express anger, frustration and sorrow before God: he can take it, and will do so willingly. Then comes a renewed submission to divine Lordship, for several psalms of lament change tone in the closing verses, shifting emphasis from expressing the pain of life to offering a fresh sacrifice of praise to the living God.

To God with Love

Why are you downcast, O my soul?
Why so disturbed within me?
Put your hope in God,
for I will yet praise him,
my Saviour and my God.

Psalm 43:5

Personal response

Are there any struggles in your life that you have been keeping away
from God? Try using a psalm of lament to pray through your blues.

6

Prayer Ministry

Just as praying for people in their absence is a natural consequence of seeking to walk in the way of love, it is also good to pray with people, both about their needs and for a fresh encounter with the love of God. Dave and Jill's first child, Sam, slept through the night for the first time when he was twenty-one months old. A month later his younger brother was born, which threw Sam's sleep pattern for another nine months. As they limped through life, constantly exhausted, Dave and Jill no longer had the faith to pray for Sam to sleep soundly. The most they could manage was a weary prayer for the strength to survive the next twenty-four hours. The prayers of others expressed a stronger faith than their own and kept them going until the final breakthrough. Similarly, those caring for an aged relative, coping with long-term unemployment or a debilitating disease can all benefit from leaning regularly upon the compassionate and faithful prayer support of others.

Insensitive and inappropriate praying is inevitably counter-productive. If those who are praying attempt to impose their own understanding of the circumstances and feelings of the person in need, or insist upon a particular response, those receiving prayer are unlikely to want to be prayed with again. Genuine and effective praying with others often has much in common with non-directive counselling skills: we assist someone as they seek to meet with the living God, bringing before him their needs, hopes and fears. All we can do is facilitate the encounter: we should strenuously avoid any kind of manipulation or pressure upon the person receiving prayer.

Such prayer requires a double listening. We must always seek to listen to the person, sensing the inner dynamic behind the presenting need or prayer request. For me, praying with eyes open is an integral part of such sensitivity, not in a manner that might suggest an over-zealous cross-examination or interrogation, but with discretion and gentleness. When we see someone's face as we pray, their expression will often give us important clues as to how their response to our prayer and to God is progressing. They may look bored and indifferent, which is usually a reliable indication not to pray much longer! Their face or hands may be taut with inner tension, stress or anxiety. They may begin to smile, weep or relax. A sudden change of facial expression may indicate that the Holy Spirit is beginning to touch their inner life, melting fears, renewing hope and restoring their soul.

At the same time, we have to learn to listen to the Spirit. There may be a Scripture to quote, a phrase from a song or hymn, a picture or a prophetic word. In my own experience, there are times when I experience a very strong impression that the Spirit is prompting me to say something specific. At other times, the first I know that the Spirit has gone far beyond the little that I can do is when someone indicates a deep response to a particular phrase or Scripture that has just been spoken. Listening to God, therefore, includes an open and submissive spirit, recognising that God alone can meet the deepest needs of the person for whom we are praying.

Eight further principles are crucial if we want to develop a sustained and effective prayer ministry in the local church, where it is surely not enough to experience an occasional display of spiritual fireworks once every few months. First, a time of prayer ministry needs to be led sensitively, so that people know clearly that someone is in control, protecting the meeting from the flesh and the devil, keeping everyone focused on Christ and his glory, and giving individuals permission to remain in their seats, request further prayer or slip out of the meeting.

Second, most of us are far less likely to be open to Christ if we feel pressured to make a particular response. There should be no hype, no manipulation. Equally, some people are frozen by the fear of disapproval: 'What might my friend think if I ask for prayer?' A healthy church will encourage a relaxed, non-critical, friendly and supportive atmosphere in which there is freedom in every meeting either to receive or not receive personal prayer. Quiet worship songs can help, encouraging people to continue to focus on the Lord in prayer, whether or not they are seeking personal ministry. The music also provides a helpful 'sound blackout' if people want to confide something personal for prayer without wanting others in the room to hear about it.

Third, many will instinctively ask the same question whenever they are faced with an opportunity for personal prayer: 'Can I trust those who are offering to pray for me?' It is important to develop a credible core team for prayer ministry in the local church, to which others can then be apprenticed. This provides a measure of accountability, training and support, and also ensures that appropriate guidelines are understood and followed. The development of a team also emphasises that this is a ministry within the body, in which believers serve one another before the Lord. We need to strenuously avoid the 'superstar' approach, in which all the praying is done by a single person. Whenever possible I travel with a prayer ministry team and I am convinced that their praying is often far more significant than my own, for a simple reason. If I did all the praying for others, people might remember me too much and the Holy Spirit too little. By seeing a team of ordinary people praying, it is much more natural for those we are visiting to conclude: 'If the Holy Spirit can work through ordinary Christians from that church, he can surely do the same through us!'

Fourth, those praying need also to receive prayer, for otherwise we suggest that there are two categories of Christians, the needy and those who have graduated to a higher plane of spiritual triumph. Just as no one should join a counselling team without experiencing at least one counselling session as a client, no one should join a prayer ministry team without first being on the receiving end of prayer. Those who continue to pray for others need also to be seen to continue to receive.

Fifth, when we pray for others, the most important thing to convey is that they are truly loved by God and also by those praying for them. Some will experience a fresh encounter with the Holy Spirit. Some will experience physical healing, a renewed sense of Christian assurance, a new inner strength in the peace of God that passes understanding. Others may experience nothing at all, or walk away from prayer with the same physical needs as before. If we pray for others because we are motivated by the love of Christ, it is absolutely crucial that the primary objective of prayer is that we convey something of the living God's amazing, holy love to them, irrespective of how 'successful' the immediate impact of our praying may or may not appear to be.

Sixth, prayer ministry needs to be provided within appropriate boundaries. These need to be agreed within the local church, but some of the elements are obvious. No cowboys: those involved in prayer ministry need to be recognised, approved and be made accountable to the church leadership team. Avoid needless sexual temptations or misunderstandings: while some churches allow men to pray for women in a public meeting, one-to-one praying in private is almost invariably unwise and asking for trouble. In many churches, the actual praying is provided in pairs: this allows the less experienced to be apprenticed into the ministry, and also encourages a sensitive complementarity, in which we can cover one another's blind spots.

Seventh, praying in a public gathering should never be allowed to become a public spectacle: there is absolutely no place for showmanship if we are praying in the love of Christ. I saw a recent TV programme in which a hyperactive preacher was leaping from one side of the room to another, laying hands upon people with such suddenness and vigour that they were thrown to the ground by the impact of his arrival. Such a circus brings great discredit to the authentic work of God: as the pushy preacher propelled others to the floor he was seeking to maintain propulsion in the pseudo-spirituality of his ministry. The overwhelming inrush of divine love or the weighty presence of divine glory can genuinely sweep people off their feet, but there is no excuse for forced reactions or an obsession with external side effects. Prayer ministry needs to be centred solely upon the glory of Christ, and never upon the antics of those doing the praying.

Eighth, and this is really the most important principle of all, prayer ministry will only be sustained as an effective ministry of the local church if the people are being fed from the Word in preaching that is faithful and reliable, envisioning and practical. Without the nourishment of good Bible teaching, prayer ministry is likely to become superficial and will eventually wither. The Word of God provides the essential ingredients for a balanced and healthy spiritual diet: when we suffer from biblical malnourishment, we risk becoming gluttons for the junk food of instant spiritual gratification. Such an approach is inevitably superficial and ultimately deeply unsatisfying. In my view this was the fatal flaw of many of the experience-centred meetings of the Welsh Revival, where preaching was sidelined and even abandoned. Since the Word always points to the Father, Son and Spirit, properly crafted biblical preaching will always stir and deepen our spiritual appetite, beckoning and inviting us to receive more deeply and to walk more closely with the Spirit of the living God to the glory of the risen Christ.

Practical response

What do you think are the three most important priorities for a local church prayer ministry team?

7

Bible Meditation

PSALM 54

Read the psalm slowly, exploring the way the psalmist moves between his themes and also moves between addressing God and addressing himself.

First comes the urgent request to be rescued (v.1–2).

Then a description of the enemies who attack him (v.3).

He affirms to himself that God is his helper (v.4).

This leads to a prayer for judgment upon his enemies (v.5).

The poet is then able to choose to offer a freewill sacrifice of praise (v.6).

Finally the poet speaks again to himself, or perhaps to others (v.7).

There has not yet been time, presumably, for the request of verse 1 to be fulfilled. But by the end of his song the psalmist views his circumstances through eyes of confident faith, declaring the consistent pattern of his life to be deliverance, thanks to his Rescuer. The crisis that had overshadowed him at the beginning of the psalm has now been overshadowed in turn by his living hope in the constant faithfulness of God.

Read the psalm aloud, entering into the changing moods of the prayer. If you cannot apply the psalm to your present circumstances, think back to a time when this kind of prayer applied to you. Alternatively, enter into the psalm on behalf of someone you know who is going through a hard time. Make this psalm into a timely prayer for them.

Poems, Prayers and Hymns for Reflection

From THE PASSING OF ARTHUR

Pray for my soul. More things are wrought by prayer
Than this world dreams of. Wherefore, let thy voice
Rise like a fountain for me night and day.
For what are men better than sheep or goats
That nourish a blind life within the brain,
If, knowing God, they lift not hands of prayer
Both for themselves and those who call them friend?
For so the whole round earth is every way
Bound by gold chains about the feet of God.

Alfred, Lord Tennyson, 1809–92

Deep peace of the Running Wave to you.
Deep peace of the Flowing Air to you.
Deep peace of the Quiet Earth to you.
Deep peace of the Shining Stars to you.
Deep peace of the Son of Peace to you.

Celtic Benediction

To God with Love

The off'rings of the Eastern kings of old
Unto our Lord were incense, myrrh and gold;
Incense because a God; gold as a king;
And myrrh as to a dying man they bring.
Instead of incense, Blessed Lord, if we
Can send a sigh or fervent prayer to thee,
Instead of myrrh if we can but provide
Tears that from penitential eyes do slide,
And though we have no gold, if for our part
We can present thee with a broken heart
Thou wilt accept: and say those Eastern kings
Did not present thee with more precious things.

Nathaniel Wanley, 1634–80

Dear Lord and Father of mankind,
Forgive our foolish ways!
Re-clothe us in our rightful mind;
In purer lives thy service find,
In deeper reverence, praise.

In simple trust like theirs who heard,
Beside the Syrian Sea,
The gracious calling of the Lord,
Let us, like them, without a word,
Rise up and follow thee.

O Sabbath rest by Galilee!
O calm of hills above,
Where Jesus knelt to share with thee
The silence of eternity,
Interpreted by love.

With that deep hush subduing all
Our words and works that drown
The tender whisper of thy call,
As noiseless let thy blessing fall
As fell thy manna down.

Drop thy still dews of quietness
Till all our strivings cease:
Take from our souls the strain and stress,
And let our ordered lives confess
The beauty of thy peace.

Breathe through the heats of our desire
Thy coolness and thy balm;
Let sense be dumb – let flesh retire;
Speak through the earthquake, wind and fire
O still small voice of calm!

John Greenleaf Whittier, 1807–92

A hymn by Charles Wesley

Where shall my wondering soul begin?
How shall I all to heaven aspire?
A slave redeemed from death and sin,
A brand plucked from eternal fire,
How shall I equal triumphs raise,
And sing my great Deliverer's praise!

O, how shall I the goodness tell,
Father, which thou to me hast showed?
That I, a child of wrath and hell,
I should be called a child of God!
Should know, should feel my sins forgiven,
Blessed with this antepast of heaven!

And shall I slight my Father's love,
Or basely fear his gifts to own?
Unmindful of his favours prove?
Shall I, the hallowed cross to shun,
Refuse his righteousness t'impart,
By hiding it within my heart?

No – though the ancient dragon rage,
And call forth all his hosts to war;
Though earth's self-righteous sons engage;
Them, and their god, alike I dare:
Jesus, the sinner's friend, proclaim;
Jesus, to sinners still the same.

Outcasts of men, to you I call,
Harlots, and publicans, and thieves!
He spreads his arms t'embrace you all;
Sinners alone his grace receive:
No need of him the righteous have,
He came the lost to seek and save.

Come, all ye Magdalenes in lust,
Ye ruffians fell in murders old;
Repent, and live: despair and trust!
Jesus for you to death was sold;
Though hell protest, and earth repine,
He died for crimes like yours – and mine.

Come, O my guilty brethren, come,
  Groaning beneath your load of sin!
His bleeding heart shall make you room,
  His open side shall take you in.
He calls you now, invites you home:
Come, O my guilty brethren, come!

For you the purple current flowed
  In pardons from his wounded side:
Languished for you th'eternal God,
  For you the Prince of Glory died.
Believe, and all your guilt's forgiven;
  Only believe – and yours is heaven.

CHAPTER V

THE PLACE OF SOLITUDE

Finding space to pray

Far from the world, O Lord, I flee,
From strife and tumult far;
From scenes, where Satan wages still
His most successful war.

The calm retreat, the silent shade,
With prayer and praise agree;
And seem by thy sweet bounty made,
For those who follow thee.

There if thy Spirit touch the soul,
And grace her mean abode;
Oh with what peace, and joy, and love,
She communes with her God!

There like the nightingale she pours
Her solitary lays;
Nor asks a witness of her song,
Nor thirsts for human praise.

Author and Guardian of my life,
Sweet source of light divine;
And (all harmonious names in one)
My Saviour; thou art mine!

What thanks I owe thee, and what love
A boundless, endless store;
Shall echo through the realms above,
When times shall be no more.

William Cowper

1

Jesus' Solitary Place

The remains of a first-century fishing jetty have been found a short distance along the shore of Lake Galilee from the ancient town of Capernaum. This is the area known as Tabgha, where a little church commemorates the miracle of the feeding of the five thousand. Several springs gush into the lake near the jetty, although those with high mineral deposits have been diverted in recent years, now that Galilee provides most of the fresh drinking water for the modern state of Israel. It seems likely that the local fishermen two thousand years ago built their jetty in this place because standing in the lake beneath the gushing springs was an ideal way to wash their nets at the end of a fishing trip.

In Capernaum the stone floor of the synagogue from the time of Jesus, where he taught and cast out a demon, can still be seen. But Capernaum itself has become an uninhabited ruin. This is a salutary warning, for Capernaum and the nearby lakeside communities were the centres of Jesus' Galilean ministry, the location for much of his preaching and healing. When the townsfolk rejected Jesus' message, he spoke prophetic words of judgment, to which today's ruins pay ominous witness.

Then Jesus began to denounce the cities in which most of his miracles had been performed, because they did not repent. 'Woe to you, Korazin! Woe to you, Bethsaida! If the miracles that were performed in you had been performed in Tyre and Sidon, they would have repented long ago in sackcloth and ashes. But I tell you, it will be more bearable for Tyre and Sidon on the day of judgment than for you. And you, Capernaum, will you be lifted up to the skies? No, you will go down to the depths. If the miracles that were performed in you had been performed in Sodom, it would have remained to this day. But I tell you that it will be more bearable for Sodom on the day of judgment than for you.'

Matthew 11:20–24

Above the jetty is a rugged hillside, too steep for the ancient dwellers in Capernaum to build upon, too stony for the local farmers to attempt to cultivate. It is a place as solitary today as it was in the time of Jesus, and known by some as Eremos, from the Greek word used in the Gospels to denote a solitary place. We cannot prove it, but it seems possible, even likely, that this was a place to which Jesus would escape from the press of the crowds. Perhaps it was from this hillside that Jesus observed the fishermen who were going to become his disciples, selecting those men with the kind of leadership potential for which he was looking. It may well have been upon this hillside that Jesus stayed to pray after feeding the five thousand, sending his disciples ahead in the boat to Bethsaida. Looking out across the lake, he saw them straining against a violent storm and then walked out on the water to still the wind and rescue them (Mark 6:45–51).

At the height of Jesus' popularity, the people gathered to hear him from many of the towns and villages around the lake. When he travelled across the lake by boat, crowds would pursue him around the shore. The demands upon Jesus were not just for more of his wonderfully vivid parables and preaching. The Gospel writers make it clear that the requests for healing and deliverance were relentless, with the needy, supported by their relatives and friends, clamouring constantly for Jesus' attention from morning till night (e.g. Mark 1:32–3).

Faced with these demands, Jesus could have worked flat out seven days a week, devoting his entire lifetime to teaching and healing among the lakeside communities. We know that this ministry was physically and emotionally exhausting, since on at least one occasion Jesus fell asleep in the boat while his disciples navigated back across the lake (Mark 4:38). Anyone who is constantly meeting new people will know just how emotionally wearing such a life can be. From Jesus' own words we also discover that he knew spiritual exhaustion, for when the woman with a haemorrhage reached out to touch him for healing he experienced 'power going out from him' (Mark 5:30).

Jesus lived the perfectly balanced life. He was not going to fall for the superficial allure of public acclaim or get sucked into celebrity status, never wanting to be absent from the public gaze. Nor was he going to become a slave to the constant demands the people placed upon him. His caring response to the crowds was both genuine and intense: the Gospel writers use a distinctive Greek word to describe Jesus' compassion, that speaks of him feeling torn apart in the guts. Alongside this intensely compassionate response to the needs of others, Jesus knew how to pace himself, recognising that the pastoral needs of these communities were a bottomless pit: whenever someone was healed or a demon cast out, another pastoral crisis was sure to be not far behind.

Jesus recognised that it was absolutely essential to ration his own availability. His method was not to send away the needy who queued at his door, but rather to take himself away to solitary places to pray. The Gospels speak of Jesus going off on his own by day and by night, in preparation for coming ministry and after the crowds' demands had left him spiritually drained. Solitary prayer was like a punctuation mark in Jesus' lifestyle, giving meaning, shape and continuing effectiveness to his public life. Removing himself from the crowds, and even from the companionship of his closest followers was an integral part of who Jesus was. He spoke of doing only what the Father set before him, and pivotal to that calling was never losing sight of the central relationship in his life: to walk in intimacy with his Father in heaven, loving him with every fibre of his being. Solitary prayer was not escapism, an indulgence, or the quirk of an unusual personality type. It was the fuel that fired his public ministry, so that wherever he taught, whomever he spoke with or healed, the compassionate love and spiritual authority of Jesus burned ever bright.

Some of the most memorable days of prayer I have ever known were spent on this solitary hillside outside Capernaum. After a hearty kibbutz breakfast I would go up on to the hillside, with a Bible, a camera and a Walkman loaded with a cassette of Mark's Gospel. The whole day stretched ahead of me, with prayer and Bible reading interrupted only by taking photographs: tranquil panoramas of the vast lake with its encircling hills, the iridescent flowers of the field to which Jesus referred in the Sermon on the Mount, the bay formed like a natural amphitheatre where Jesus may have preached from a fishing boat, the huge thistles and barren, rocky places of the kind Jesus probably pointed at when telling the parable of the sower. Far below me, down by the lake, the tour parties continued to clock up their hasty visits, rushing through the historic places to complete their itinerary, often pausing less to reflect or pray than to drive a hard bargain for souvenir pottery and olive-wood carvings. High on the hillside, for undisturbed hours I explored the sheer pleasure of being alone with God, walking in Jesus' footsteps and learning from his example. If Jesus frequently needed to remove himself from the crowds and his friends for time alone with God, our need for solitude is surely at least as great, in the constant, frenetic rush of the modern world.

Practical reflection

Withdrawal for solitary prayer can provide the punctuation marks in the story of our lives. Do we need to insert more commas and full stops into our busy schedules?

2

Paul's Hidden Years

The apostle Paul knew hidden years at the beginning and end of his ministry. After his dramatic conversion, a superficial reading of Acts 9 might suggest that it was within a few days of his arrival that the Christians had to extricate him from the city concealed in a basket. Certainly Paul, or Saul as he was still known at this time, spent several days with the disciples in Damascus as soon as he arrived, preaching in the synagogues that Jesus is nothing less than the Son of God (Acts 9:19–22). At the beginning of verse 23 Luke passes swiftly over an intervening period with the phrase 'after many days had gone by'. That is, 'several days' were spent in the city, followed by 'many days' elsewhere. Before this hidden period, Luke describes the believers in Damascus as 'disciples'. After Paul's return to the city, they have become 'his followers' (v.25).

Paul tells us more about this hidden period in his letter to the Galatians. He explains that he quickly left Damascus and went into Arabia. It was only after his return to Damascus that Paul eventually travelled back to Jerusalem, some three years later. This brought about his first meeting with Peter and James and his first contact with the church in that city (Gal. 1:17–19).

Paul emphasises a striking contrast between his life before and after conversion. Before, he was a self-made man, establishing a vigorous career path among the professional elite of Judaism. He was advancing beyond his years, extremely fervent in his knowledge and defence of Jewish traditions, and taking a lead in the persecution of the followers of Jesus. He was not only zealous, but *seen* to be zealous; winning the approval of others for his efforts seems to have always been extremely important to him. He was a young man with brilliant prospects ahead of him (Gal. 1:13–14).

After his conversion, Paul was overwhelmingly aware not of his own career prospects, but of Christ's call upon his life to preach the good news among the Gentiles. Far from courting the approval of established leaders in his accustomed manner, he deliberately delayed making any contact with them at all (Gal. 1:16–19). This was not arrogance, but submission. Paul chose the path of hiddenness, not announcing prematurely his call to be an apostle, but rather withdrawing, in order to lay the wise preparation of a secure foundation. He no longer lusted after status or approval: what mattered was not to be noticed by men and women but to live in such a way as to be a servant of Christ and to please God (Gal. 1:10).

The novels of Austen, Dickens and Trollope are littered with clergymen who are pursuing a religious career, courting favour in the eyes of men. Sometimes today we encounter gifted speakers or celebrity converts with a public ministry that risks being little more than a five-minute wonder. We can rush people into a premature prominence when they lack the spiritual depth and maturity to cope. Like an extravagant firework display, they illuminate the sky with wondrous pyrotechnics and then, just as quickly, their public ministry fades away into dust and ashes.

Paul does not tell us what he did during the hidden years, but it is not difficult to identify three priorities. First, he studied the Scriptures. There was never a hint of an illuminist in Paul, never a desire to stop studying the Scriptures or to cease using his mind once he had encountered the risen Christ and entered into a new life. When Paul got up from the Damascus road, there was no suggestion that he would now dispense with his Old Testament scrolls. Far from it, for he devoured them afresh in the coming years. His preaching and his letters are full of Old Testament quotations, for he learnt to study the Jewish Scriptures as a prophetic anticipation and preparation for Christ, finding their fulfilment in his life, death, resurrection and promised return.

Second, Paul must surely have spent much time in prayer. He makes no apology in his letters for regularly encouraging believers to find time to pray and regularly telling them how much they are in his prayers. The great foundation for the tremendous vigour and zeal of his future ministry was laid in the stillness of prayer.

The third great factor in Paul's hidden years was to devote his brilliant mind to rigorous reflection on the meaning of the cross and its implications for evangelism among the Gentiles. Many Jewish Christians made the automatic and unthinking assumption that if Gentiles were to be converted they would need to conform to Judaism, accepting circumcision and the complete set of obligations laid out in the Torah. Paul's letter to the Galatians may be his earliest great study of the impact of the cross and the absolute incompatibility between the legalistic approach of the Judaisers and a complete dependence upon the atoning sacrifice of Christ. In human terms, it was largely thanks to the theological precision of Paul's thinking about the cross that Gentile converts were given exemption from the Jewish law and treated as full and equal partners in the new people of God.

At the end of his ministry and also in his previous imprisonments, Paul tasted a second hiddenness. Some Christians deserted him, presumably because they feared for their own lives (2 Tim. 4:16). Others may have wondered whether he was a genuine apostle when the Lord allowed him to remain under house arrest. He suffered under these privations, missing free access to the scrolls he loved to study and the pleasure of the company of his friends (2 Tim. 4:9–13). Nonetheless, Paul's eyes remained fixed on Christ and his service. He spoke of himself as Christ's slave (Phil. 1:1), rejoiced that his imprisonment had served the advance of the gospel (Phil 1:12), and encouraged his fellow Christians to continue to serve one another in love and shine like the stars in witness to the Lordship of Christ (Phil. 2:1–16).

As to Paul's own priorities, he explained that, above all else, his life was devoted to one thing: 'the surpassing greatness of knowing Christ Jesus my Lord' (Phil. 3:8). In the hiddenness of imprisonment, uncertain whether he might be facing imminent execution, Paul declared that he willingly embraced not only the 'power of his resurrection' but also the 'fellowship of sharing in his sufferings' (Phil. 3:10). This was not serving Christ as an obedient servant at a remote distance. Out of an intimate closeness to his master and a living experience of walking in the Spirit, Paul accepted with great courage the prospect of imminent martyrdom. The remarkable strength of mind and character that Paul demonstrates in his prison letters is surely grounded in that earlier experience of hidden years in Arabia. Paul had learnt the art of investing in his ultimate concern, taking time out from the constant demands and opportunities of an active life in order to continue to cultivate a deepening inner relationship with Christ.

Personal evaluation

Are there times when you have rushed into action, but on reflection it would have been wiser first to have taken time out for prayerful preparation?

3

Obsessed with Productivity

A Christian solicitor received a written evaluation following his annual review. His workload and effectiveness were exemplary. No one could dispute that he was dedicated and successful. However, he had made a resolve not to make a habit of regularly working late in the office, believing that he should also give due priority to his responsibilities as a father of young children and as a husband. The final evaluation was dismissive: 'He lacks commitment.'

A more holistic evaluation would have drawn a quite different conclusion: 'He is pursuing a well-considered balancing of his commitments to work and to family life.' Sadly, in many companies in Britain today, a wider, holistic understanding of life is completely lacking. Annual appraisal has been treated not as a way of sustaining rounded personal development, but rather as a means of extracting ever more hours of work. We live in a period when there is a high underlying rate of unemployment in the economy, and yet, at the same time, many of those in work are working longer hours than ever before.

As Christians we surely need to make a double objection to this trend. First, life is meant to be about far more than work, and to compel ever-longer hours is nothing less than exploitation, whether the demands are being imposed upon unskilled manual workers or highly paid professionals. Second, longer hours do not necessarily mean greater productivity: in the short term, the breathing space of leisure and family time can sustain a sense of freshness and creativity in the workplace; in the medium term, a life narrowly lived within the confines of work will frequently lead to burn out and breakdowns. A rising suicide rate among men in their twenties may indicate that a terrible price is beginning to be paid for the ruthless imposition of ever-longer working hours and ever-greater pressure in the workplace. My own hope is that an increasing number of Christians will have the courage to establish businesses built around a more biblical and holistic set of values. The long-term well-being of both the company and its employees is ultimately more important than squeezing out every last drop of profitability in the current year. Those who live by the short-term bottom line are increasingly likely to die by the short-term bottom line.

We can all get sucked into a cultural mindset in which it feels as if there is never enough time. Life is lived against the clock, always in a rush, always juggling priorities. To be over-pressed has become a virtue, to be busy is the minimum requirement, and so to be at rest is an indulgence, a damning indictment of personal indolence. You can see this in the way people walk in modern cities: everyone is in haste as the relentless seconds tick away. Even watching television can take on workaholic tendencies. Some never watch a programme without doing something else at the same time because relaxation would be an unjustifiable waste of time. Others surf the channels, attempting to follow several programmes at once in order to squeeze a little more activity into an existence permanently short of time. Like the White Rabbit in *Alice in Wonderland*, we are continually in a hurry, and often, quite literally, running late.

Children frequently become the greatest victims of a workaholic culture. There was a time when parents might pay for one evening activity for their young children each week: at other times they were free to indulge that most privileged of childhood activities, imaginative play. Now the great tyrant of constant productivity holds childhood in its grip. For many children of primary school age, not a single evening passes without some kind of self-improvement for which their parents have paid: Monday is the piano, Tuesday tuition in maths, Wednesday football training, Thursday tuition in English, and Friday the trumpet. In this relentless quest for the ambitions of adults to be fulfilled vicariously through their children I have two questions. First, can any child be expected to succeed when stretched in so many directions at once? And second, are the parents so driven, so obsessed with the need to achieve, that they are no longer prepared to allow their offspring the time simply to be children? When achievement is everything, whatever has happened to fun, laughter and imaginative play?

A workaholic, attainment-driven culture is hostile not only to the innocent pleasures of childhood, but also to prayer. For those living in the now, with a constant backlog of deadlines on their daily to-do list, there may never be any free space in the diary during which to pray. Prayer has no sense of priority; it seems an indulgence, lacking a contribution to productivity. And so prayer gets squeezed to the margins, or even disappears.

This should not surprise us, for behind the materialism of an acquisitive society lies the philosophical framework of secular materialism. A governing supposition of this value system that has increasingly shaped Western society throughout the twentieth century is the conviction that spirituality is surplus to requirements, an obsolete hangover from a more superstitious age. Individuals are naturally free to indulge such traditional activities if they really must, so long as their eccentricity is kept strictly to the private domain. Spirituality is marginalised as an optional extra, for those who have a weakness or penchant for that sort of thing. It has no right to intrude into the public world of business, politics or education. Christian prayer is treated as no more significant than any other hobby or pastime, no more relevant to the public life of the nation, the boardroom or the hours we work than keeping goldfish or collecting stamps.

Christians can easily succumb to this dualism, this pressure to 'keep the sacred out of the secular'. On the one hand, those who are involved in leadership at work, where they have great expertise in strategic planning, goal setting and team building, may feel that their skills are somehow 'unspiritual' and irrelevant to the life of the church. Simultaneously, a lack of integration can mean that committed Christians fail to think and live Christianly in the workplace, neither applying biblical principles to business ethics nor finding time to pray. We get sucked into the workaholism of the world, but the pressure may seem even worse for the dedicated believer, because we additionally have to squeeze all our church activities into a life that is already far too frenetic. Bill Hybels has used a telling phrase to reverse this mindset that marginalises prayer: 'Too busy not to pray.'

I went away for some days of prayer with another Christian leader, who told me that the last time he took such a break he came back with a bulky report setting out many new proposals for his organisation to implement. I am by no means against vision building: part of our calling is to dream dreams of how we can serve Christ more effectively. However, I set a challenge before my friend: 'If you have come away to write a new vision statement, that's fine. But if you have taken time out simply to be with the Lord, then I suggest you use these days to seek his presence and not to write a five-year plan. If this is time set aside to walk in the presence of the Lord, then I invite you to resolve right now that you intend to go home with no new proposals, no new plans at all.'

Naturally, the living God reserves the right to give us new plans and dreams when we are seeking his presence. My fear was that my friend was tempted to justify his days of prayer by an immediate demonstration upon his return of his prodigious productivity. Taking time out with Jesus is not only about action, but also effectiveness; it's about *being with Christ* before *doing for Christ.* Who we are in Christ, as we learn to take time out to practise his presence, makes an incalculable long-term difference not only to what we do, but even more to how we do it. This is far from suggesting that we should completely abandon being active in Christian service, for no Christian has ever achieved more in three years than did Jesus. But the remarkable authority and impact of Jesus' public ministry was incalculably enhanced by the discipline of regular withdrawal into solitude. Solitary prayer is the hidden engine-room of effectual Christian living.

Personal reflection

Have you ever felt trapped on a treadmill, running flat out but getting nowhere? What circumstances put you there and how can you decisively break the pattern?

4

Places of the Presence

Some places are permeated with a holy presence. This is not mere superstition, for many people sense the presence in the same places. For many visitors to the Holy Land, Jerusalem is the great disappointment and Galilee the great delight. Jerusalem is one of the most religious cities on the face of the earth. Although Jews and Muslims are the two largest religious groupings, there are plenty of Christians, not only a significant minority among the Palestinians and the Armenian people, but also the resident representatives of many Christian traditions. The major Christian holy sites of Jerusalem are often the joint responsibility of several denominations, and sometimes their understanding of Christian unity seems more to do with maintaining an unhealthy and all too obvious rivalry than with the pursuit of constructive co-operation. Such attitudes are hardly conducive to a sense of the holy presence.

Jerusalem today is a vibrant, hustling, noisy city, teeming with traders, with arguments and ethnic tensions. It is an unforgettable city, of remarkably ancient lineage, but it is a city distinguished more by the excesses of human religion than by any distinctive sense of the holy presence. Perhaps this should not surprise us: Jerusalem was the city over which Jesus mourned, for its people and authorities had rejected and killed many prophets, and within a few days they would do the same to Jesus (Matt. 23:37). It is the city of the resurrection of Jesus and the gift of the Spirit, but it is also the city of his rejection and cross.

Much of Galilee remains undeveloped. Although Tiberias has become an impersonal, modern tourist town and many kibbutzim have been established around the lake, the lake is still fairly quiet and the surrounding countryside remains unspoilt. The physical environment of the time of Jesus is remarkably well preserved, so that those who take time out from the express itineraries of the tourist trail can still enter into a profound experience of walking in the Master's footsteps. The same is true of the lake itself. A first-century fishing boat was found well preserved in the lakeside mud and from it a replica has been made. The modern vessel has a petrol engine, not least for safety reasons, but once far out from the shore, with the engine turned off and the sails up, surrounded by the vast stillness of the lake, today's visitors can enter into the sights and sounds of the time of Jesus to an uncanny degree.

In Britain, many Christians continue to benefit from visiting the isolated, ancient centres of Christian prayer at Lindisfarne and Iona. Perhaps it is simply the rugged beauty of these places, or perhaps there really is something more. To have been centres of worship, prayer and mission for so long seems to have imbued these places with a remarkable sense of God's immanence. Iona has been called a 'thin place' because the distance there between heaven and earth seems unusually slender. Lindisfarne came to be known as Holy Island. Many speak of being stirred to prayer with an unmistakable awareness of standing on ground made holy by the divine presence. Aidan's prayer for Lindisfarne seeks to express the sense of a place that has been soaked in Christian devotion:

> *Here be the peace of those who do your will;*
> *Here be the peace of brother serving other;*

The Place of Solitude

Here be the peace of holy monks obeying:
Here be the peace of praise by night and day.

For me, an ancient place of prayer almost overwhelmingly touched by the divine is Rievaulx Abbey in the North Yorkshire moors. Admittedly it was a more forbidding place when wolves still roamed the surrounding forests, and the wild harshness of winter in the moors is nothing like the balmy days of summer when tourists flock to the site today. These monks were no ascetics, for the glorious beauty of the valley where they chose to settle is more than matched by the exquisite delicacy of their buildings. One of the most beautiful ruins in England, every soaring arch lifts the human spirit in fresh songs of praise. With the centre of prayer and learning, the monks of Rievaulx also established a highly successful farming business. This great combination of spirituality, learning and commercial expertise indicates a remarkably integrated and holistic vision of abundant life in Christ. Devoting quality time to prayer, far from disqualifying believers from making a significant contribution in other dimensions of life, can actually equip and release us into a greater, all-round effectiveness.

A centre of prayer does not have to become an ancient ruin before it can be imbued with the divine presence. Nearly twenty years ago, when Claire and I first visited Lee Abbey, the Christian conference centre on the North Devon coast, we both remarked upon an amazing and unforgettable awareness of God as we walked in the grounds. Later we discovered that members of the Lee Abbey community were committed to praying specifically for the divine presence throughout their estate. Soaking with prayer had made this far more than a Christian centre. It too had become a holy place, a place of the divine presence.

For me personally, a place does not need to have been a centre of Christian prayer to become imbued with the divine presence.

Some of my most intimate, life-enriching seasons of encounter with God have been in the fells, beside mountain streams, or standing on high cliffs far above the sea's crashing waves. To be alone amidst the extravagant beauty of creation, feeling so very dwarfed by the vast forces of wind, water and earth, these are moments to sense the wordless eloquence of the song of creation and to join in that cosmic hymn of praise. These are moments also to sense the Creator's approval, when he sees his handiwork undisfigured by human exploitation. As the living God continues to enjoy the glorious, harmonious beauty that has been fashioned by his love, still the Creator is able to declare, and we with him: 'It is very good!' (Gen. 1:31).

An unforgettable opportunity to enter into someone else's sense of a holy place arose the first time I visited Wastwater, on the western outskirts of the English Lake District. It is a remote, desolate and awe-inspiring place, quite unlike the verdant beauty of the better-known lakes. Towering above the still waters are mighty – and potentially deadly – scree runs. The tumbled stones and rocky outcrops run far down beneath the surface of the lake. It is a place that seems uncanny, other-worldly, carrying with it even a sense of foreboding and dread. As I stood there, gazing at this terrible beauty, a couple turned towards me and one of them spoke: 'We love to stand here,' she said. 'To us it's a glimpse of heaven.' At first I was shocked that they should see anything of heaven in a place so inhospitable to men and women. Then I began to enter into their experience, for they recognised a beauty that served a higher end than human usefulness. In the sense of dread and awe that Wastwater's barren heights evoke, I think they sensed a fear and trembling before the transcendent, majestic otherness of God.

Personal reflection

Do you have any holy places, to which it would be good to return soon?

5

A Personal Place of Withdrawal

A national survey in Britain in 1997 sought to identify common
factors in marriages that survive and stay healthy. One frequent
response was decidedly unexpected: a garden shed. It seems that,
for many British men, a garden shed is somewhere to escape, a
place of hiddenness and relaxation. In these days of equality, in
many households both husband and wife go out to work, and so
the house is presumably becoming less the woman's domain than
once it was. Perhaps this means that in future garden sheds will
begin to be sold in pairs – his and hers – so that both partners
are able to preserve a sense of private space!

This need for private space is deep and instinctive, whether it
takes the form of a home office, a study, a den or, indeed, a garden
shed. Just as many of us experience the benefit of somewhere that
is just for us, somewhere to express our individuality, I believe
that the discipline of solitary prayer is greatly helped by finding
somewhere to pray without disturbance. For some, of course,
this may simply be impossible. There may be no spare room, no
garden, no access to anywhere with a measure of privacy. Others
may be enjoying or enduring the privilege of small children, with
no escape in their waking moments from a constant stream of
fresh demands. Nonetheless, if we are prepared to look hard
enough, many of us can find a private place of prayer.

For many, a spare bedroom fills the purpose, once everyone else in the household understands that you have no wish to be disturbed whenever you enter that room with a Bible rather than a Hoover. For me, the garden is often a wonderfully rewarding place to pray, so long as I restrict myself to pulling up not more than a handful of weeds. The luxuriant beauty of plants is a great stimulus to express thankfulness to the Creator. This does mean, of course, that I often pray with eyes open, while walking around. As I explained in a previous chapter, I personally find it helpful to engage the body while praying rather than park it in neutral as if our bodily existence and senses are incapable of contributing to our spiritual awareness and growth.

A friend of mine who is a pastor told me recently that he has taken to booking a room at a convent for private prayer every Friday morning. He keeps a strict discipline, choosing to make himself unavailable at that time for any meetings either within or beyond his parish. It is a time of spiritual recharging which he protects scrupulously. 'I could not possibly give up this time,' he explained, 'because it nourishes and equips me for the coming week.'

Most people's circumstances do not permit such a strict weekly regime. But perhaps there is a place for setting aside a weekend or even a day for prayer once every quarter, whether in a private place of prayer at home, by visiting a holy place or simply by spending some time out in the countryside. The vast majority of people in the developed world live in cities, and the proportion is likely to increase. When we return to the unspoilt beauty of the countryside there can be a sense of coming home, of returning to a setting for which we were created. Where at all possible, city-dwellers need to escape from time to time, and meet with God in the harmony and beauty of creation.

When we consider how to establish a private place where we can withdraw for undisturbed prayer, we need to recognise one of the great tyrants of modern living – the telephone. In many households, there is a knee-jerk reaction: when the phone rings, we have been conditioned to drop everything and rush to answer its imperious demands. Cordless and mobile phones make it worse, for it seems there is no place left to escape telephonic interruptions. Many children become accustomed to the fact that no meal passes without one of their parents being called away to yet another phone conversation. The message this conveys is unambiguous: while the children matter enough to sit down to a meal with them, whoever makes a phone call invariably matters more. In some families the best way for children to have an uninterrupted conversation with their parents would be to phone them surreptitiously from the meal table!

The common justification for this headlong rush to the phone is that it might be a really urgent or important call. This probably goes back to the early days of phones, when only a few people had them and a phone call was a momentous and unusual event. In most homes, the number of calls that are really urgent is minimal. Our hasty response, dropping everything to stop the phone ringing, is out of all proportion to the likely content of the call. Most phone calls are pleasant but trivial: a delayed response rarely makes any difference at all. I therefore suggest the following principle: if the call is desperately urgent, and you don't have an answerphone, they will either call someone else or phone you again in twenty minutes. For children we need to establish a clear sense of priority: at the meal table their company matters to us far more than whoever is trying to phone us, and so we will choose to ignore the insistent ringing. In prayer we need a similar single-mindedness: if this is my protected time in solitary prayer, it is more important to be alone with God than to answer that call. It's time to regain control over the tyranny of the telephone.

Practical evaluation

Would you benefit from establishing some kind of private space for solitary prayer? If so, where?

6

Cultivating Detachment

The New Testament never suggests that it is wrong to have or enjoy good things. But if our heart becomes too wrapped up in possessions, our spirit begins to wither. As Jesus warned, where our treasure is, our heart will be also (Matt. 6:21). In previous ages, people's self-image tended to be constructed around their social background, their thinking or their achievements. These traditional approaches brought their own problems, but today's consumerism is promoting a radical superficiality in our sense of self: we become what we buy.

Modern political leaders, not only in the United States but in Britain too, receive enormously expensive advice from image consultants on just what kind of clothes, shoes, hairstyle and even what tone of voice needs to be assumed in order to invent an image that maximises vote-winning potential.

Sometimes we are voting less for a genuine person than a designer's mannequin, dressed to win in an artfully constructed public persona. This creeping artificiality is no longer confined to pop idols, film stars and TV celebrities: post-modernism is inviting the masses to indulge in the regular re-invention of self, re-defining who we are by re-fashioning the surface of our lives. We are being invited to construct a series of new, off-the-peg identities.

If our sense of self is critically dependent upon what we buy – whether a Ferrari or the latest designer clothes and trainers – we cannot afford to be parted from those things that have established or defined our identity. Our society urgently needs to discover a deeper sense of self, where we truly find ourselves not in a public image constructed by a design consultant, but in the cultivation of our spirituality, pursuing an intimacy and stillness with our Father in heaven. If we make material possessions our ultimate concern, we place our spiritual well-being in grave danger. We need instead to learn how to place material concerns on one side, to keep them firmly in their place, so that Christ alone is the determining priority in the way we choose to live. John of the Cross issued a stark warning about the failure to cultivate the discipline of detachment:

> *Some persons, laden with wealth ... make no progress nor come to harbour, because they have not the courage to break from some whim, attachment or affection ... Yet all they have to do is to set sail resolutely, cut the ship's cable or rid themselves of the sucking fish of desire.*
>
> John of the Cross, *The Ascent of Mount Carmel,* 1:xi:iv

We need to cultivate a detachment, not only from our possessions, but also from our circumstances. The discipline of withdrawal requires an attitude of detachment. We have to learn how to switch off, at least temporarily, from the many concerns of life. We need to cultivate a sense of sharply defined focus, so that we live with a clear understanding of what matters most. In words of haunting beauty, the prophet Habakkuk expressed this sense of sharp focus and disciplined detachment, describing his resolve to give due praise to God, irrespective of the uncertainties and hazards of life as a subsistence farmer:

> *Though the fig tree does not bud*
> *and there are no grapes on the vines,*
> *though the olive crop fails*
> *and the fields produce no food,*
> *though there are no sheep in the pen*
> *and no cattle in the stalls,*
> *yet I will rejoice in the* LORD,
> *I will be joyful in God my Saviour.*
> Habakkuk 3:17–18

Detachment from circumstances must also involve a detachment from the emotions of disappointment. We need to learn how to choose to offer a sacrifice of praise as an act of will. We may not feel like rejoicing in the Lord, but he always remains worthy of our praise. Whether such impressions arise from depression or from an inexplicable spiritual dryness, still we will benefit from the discipline of solitary prayer, taking time out before the living God, both to give thanks and to continue to seek the divine presence.

When Paul was under house arrest, it must have seemed like the ultimate frustration of all his aspirations as an apostle, no longer able to preach the gospel without constraint, teach Christians, or plant and strengthen churches. However, when Paul wrote to the Philippians he was able to explain that this apparent disaster had turned out for the good (Phil. 1:12–14). First, because other Christians had been provoked into more public and active witness in his absence. Second, because the entire palace guard had ended up hearing the gospel. It seems that Paul had different soldiers chained to his wrists day by day, and he had determined to take advantage of this opportunity of a captive audience to tell them, one by one, the good news of Jesus Christ.

Matthew Henry described a 'Divine Alchemy' in the life of

the apostle Paul. Just as the alchemists sought to manufacture gold out of what they considered the four essential elements, air, fire, water and earth, the living God can create pure spiritual gold out of the most unpromising personal circumstances. When faced with disappointment or adversity, when we feel almost overcome by our situation, we need to learn how to withdraw for private prayer. And in prayer we can ask this question, 'Lord, what Divine Alchemy will you work, to bring something good out of my condition, that even in my present circumstances I may serve you to the full?'

Personal meditation

If there was a fire in your home, what is the first possession you would rush to retrieve? Pause to ensure that it functions as a servant in your life, and has not become your master.

7

Bible Meditation

MARK 1:29–39

Consider the enormous demands of Jesus' day. He comes back to Simon and Andrew's house after deliverance ministry in the synagogue. Immediately another pastoral need is presented and he provides healing for Simon's mother-in-law. No sooner have they enjoyed their supper than the whole town begins to gather at the door, bringing all their sick and demonised. By the end of this prolonged and unplanned ministry, Jesus must be exhausted.

The next morning, when most of us would be wanting to enjoy a well-deserved extra hour or two of sleep, Jesus gets up very early. While it is still dark he leaves Capernaum for Eremos, the solitary place where he can pray undisturbed. Later that morning the disciples come looking for him and inform him that the people are expecting further ministry. Jesus explains that it is time to move on: his task is to preach in turn in every village throughout Galilee.

Consider all the reasons against Jesus setting aside this time to withdraw for solitary prayer. He was tired, and needed a good rest. The people were wanting more, and it would be unfair to desert them. His disciples didn't know where he was going, and he ought to stay with them in order to look after his closest followers. He was about to begin travelling from village to village, and so he really could not afford the time to pray. Despite these persuasive objections, Jesus remained dedicated to the priority of solitary prayer.

Now consider the circumstances of your life, and all the reasons why the discipline of solitary prayer is inappropriate at present. Reflect on whether the example of Jesus may be inviting you to break free from the remorseless demands of modern existence, taking time out to be with your Master. For Jesus, prayer was never a distraction. It was the only sensible way to gather the necessary spiritual resources to accomplish all the tasks that the Father was setting before him.

Poems, Prayers and Hymns for Reflection

CONTENTMENT
He that is down needs fear no fall;
He that is low, no pride;
He that is humble, ever shall
Have God to be his guide.
I am content with what I have,
Little be it, or much:
And, Lord, contentment still I crave,
Because thou savest such.

John Bunyan, 1628–88

WHAT MORE DOTH THE LORD REQUIRE OF THEE?
To love our God with all our strength and will;
To covet nothing; to devise no ill
Against our neighbours; to procure or do
Nothing to others which we would not to
Our very selves; not to revenge our wrong;
To be content with little; not to long
For wealth and greatness; to despise or jeer
No man, and, if we be despised, to bear;

Walking with God

To feed the hungry; to hold fast our crown;
To take from others nought; to give our own,
  These are his precepts, and, alas, in these
  What is so hard but faith can do with ease?
                              Henry Vaughan, 1622–95

Lord Jesus,
may the sweet burning ardour of your love
absorb my soul entirely
and make it a stranger
to all that is not you or for you.
                    Francis of Assisi, 1181–1226

Be, Lord Jesus, a bright flame before me,
  Be a guiding star above me,
  Be a smooth path below me,
  Be a kindly shepherd behind me,
  Today, tonight, and for ever.
                        Columba of Iona, 521–97

Rock of Ages, cleft for me,
  Let me hide myself in thee;
  Let the water and the blood,
From thy riven side which flowed,
  Be of sin the double cure –
Cleanse me from its guilt and power.

The Place of Solitude

Not the labour of my hands
    Can fulfil thy law's demands:
Could my zeal no respite know,
Could my tears for ever flow,
    All for sin could not atone;
Thou must save, and thou alone.

Nothing in my hand I bring,
    Simply to thy cross I cling:
Naked, come to thee for dress;
Helpless, look to thee for grace;
    Foul, I to the fountain fly:
Wash me, Saviour, or I die!

While I draw this fleeting breath,
    When my eyelids close in death,
When I soar to worlds unknown,
See thee on thy judgment throne:
    Rock of Ages, cleft for me,
    Let me hide myself in thee!
                Augustus Toplady, 1740–78

A hymn by Charles Wesley

Thou hidden source of calm repose
    Thou all-sufficient love divine
My help, and refuge from my foes,
    Secure I am, if thou art mine,
And lo! From sin, and grief and shame
    I hide me, Jesus, in thy name.

Thy mighty name salvation is,
And keeps my happy soul above;
Comfort it brings, and power, and peace,
And joy, and everlasting love:
To me with thy dear name are given
Pardon, and holiness, and heaven.

Jesu, my all in all thou art,
My rest in toil, my ease in pain,
The medicine of my broken heart,
In war my peace, in loss my gain,
My smile beneath the tyrant's frown,
In shame my glory, and my crown.

In want my plentiful supply,
In weakness my almighty power,
In bonds my perfect liberty,
My light in Satan's darkest hour,
In grief my joy unspeakable,
My life in death, my heaven in hell.

CHAPTER VI

OPEN TO GOD

Learning to receive

Jesus, where'er thy people meet,
There they behold thy mercy-seat:
Where'er they seek thee, thou art found,
And every place is hallowed ground.

For thou, within no walls confined,
Inhabitest the humble mind:
Such ever bring thee where they come,
And going, take thee to their home.

Great Shepherd of thy chosen few,
Thy former mercies here renew;
Here to our waiting hearts proclaim
The sweetness of thy saving name.

Here may we prove the power of prayer,
To strengthen faith, and sweeten care;
To teach our faint desires to rise,
And bring all heaven before our eyes.

Lord, we are few, but thou art near,
Nor short thine arm, nor deaf thine ear;
O rend the heavens, come quickly down,
And make a thousand hearts thine own.

William Cowper

1

Humbling before God

We are destined to make little spiritual progress if we fail to learn how to humble ourselves before God. Humbling begins with a realistic grasp of our creatureliness as we come before the Creator.

In our mortality, we need to recognise that our earthly existence is a gracious but temporary gift from God, who has the right and the power to remove the gift of life at any time. In our fallibility, we come to the all-seeing, all-knowing God: his wisdom is perfect, while the best of our insights are partial, fragmentary and flawed.

Jesus emphasised that humble dependence upon God's resources is the essential prerequisite to spiritual fruitfulness: 'Apart from me you can do nothing' (John 15:5). Our immediate instinct all too often is to finalise our own plans and then ask for God's help and blessing, reducing the Holy Spirit to the role of chief cheerleader in our lives. For Christ, being comes before doing, and our actions will only be effective inasmuch as we have first learned to come to him in trust, submission and willing dependence. If we long to be effective in bearing fruit for Christ, we must learn to cultivate the living relationship of abiding in him – 'Neither can you bear fruit unless you remain in me' (John 15:4).

Paul experienced an instantaneous humbling on the Damascus road. So self-assured in his religious service, he was confident that the persecution of Christians was guaranteed to win him the favour of men and God. Once his life had been revolutionised by the risen Christ he viewed his life from a totally different perspective. To the Philippians, Paul listed the hallmarks of his racial and spiritual pedigree: by birth and by personal devotion he was outstanding among the Jews, with many qualities that set him apart:

> *If anyone else thinks he has reason to put confidence in the flesh, I have more: circumcised on the eighth day, of the people of Israel, of the tribe of Benjamin, a Hebrew of the Hebrews; in regard to the law, a Pharisee; as for zeal, persecuting the church; as for legalistic righteousness, faultless.*

> Philippians 3:4–6

For many people, this combination of a privileged birthright and outstanding achievements would be quite sufficient status in which to bask for the rest of life. Such an exceptional combination would normally result in a remarkably strong, distinguished and superior sense of self. Paul's settled conviction that salvation has been made available through faith in Christ alone leaves no place for self-congratulation or smug superiority. He explains that all these qualities and achievements are counted as loss compared to knowing Christ. More than that, he counts them as 'rubbish' (Phil. 3:7–9). A social and religious pedigree second to none, that would have been the envy of many, is dismissed out of hand. Once Christ has seized him, Paul has no time for such things. Literally, he says they have become like *dung* to him. An exemplary pedigree and an outstanding set of personal achievements are not worth touching with a bargepole, compared with living for Christ. Paul explains that although he has lost 'everything', his old social status and his career prospects among the Pharisees, he nonetheless considers himself a winner. This path of humbling really does make enormous sense, for what we gain is nothing less than devotion and surrender to the living Christ.

Humbling is a much broader aspect of our relationship with God than confession. It's not only because we commit sin that we come before Christ in humility, but also because of our creaturely dependence and, left to our own resources, our spiritual ineffectiveness. Just as Paul discovered a new humility in repudiating the merits of his social and religious pedigree, he also walked in humility with regard to his Christian lifestyle. Twice he emphatically insisted to the Philippians that he had not arrived as a Christian, dismissing as nonsense the suggestion that a respected apostle must surely have attained sinless perfection (Phil. 3:12, 13).

Even as humility was a necessary ingredient of his conversion and initial repentance, Paul recognised that, if he was to continue to grow in Christ, he needed to continue on a humble path. His spiritual well-being and effectiveness in ministry required an accurate sense of self. There were never any exaggerated claims about his own ministry or the slightest hint of self-importance. How sad that the promotion of some Christian ministries and conferences today has apparently forgotten or abandoned the principle of humility. Perhaps that's why, despite the hype, there is usually a good deal less effectiveness and fruitfulness than in Paul's ministry.

In his first letter, Peter encourages us to cultivate a continuing disposition of humility:

Humble yourselves, therefore, under God's mighty hand, that he may lift you up in due time.

1 Peter 5:6

James commends the same priority:

> *Humble yourselves before the Lord, and he will lift you up.*
>
> James 4:10

For Peter in particular this approach to life was nothing less than revolutionary. A born leader, all his natural instincts were centred on self-assertion. He thought he knew himself as a man of natural courage when he roundly rebuked Jesus for suggesting that he was heading for an early death by crucifixion in Jerusalem. With his threefold denial of his Master after he was seized in the city, Peter hit rock bottom, discovering unknown and unexpected depths of personal cowardice. As he ran out weeping into the night, Peter had not only lost his dearest friend to the imperial courts, he had also lost belief in himself. When the risen Christ appeared to Peter, he was visiting a broken man, restoring hope in one who had discovered humility through extreme failure. Peter's entire understanding of leadership and life was transformed by the way of the cross. A man who had always been eager to assert himself now urged Christians in every dimension of life, at home and at work as well as with fellow Christians, to ensure that their lifestyle gave clear expression to the serving, self-giving humility of Christ (1 Pet. 2:13–5:11).

Both James and Peter promise a new dimension to life into which we can only enter after we have learned to humble ourselves before God. While our task is to humble ourselves, in due season God will lift us up. Two principles govern this elevation of believers. First, it is God who does the lifting up, and so we are never entitled to abandon the path of humility and engage in a season of self-exaltation. Second, the timing of this exaltation is entirely in God's hands, with no guarantee that the lifting will follow quickly on the heels of the humbling. Ours, in other words, is only to choose to humble ourselves before

God, without the slightest hint of impatience if God chooses a prolonged delay before he begins to lift us up.

Several years ago I woke up in the middle of the night and went downstairs to pray. As I turned to 1 Peter 5, verse 6 stood out from the page as if written in letters of fire. I knew that I needed to pray the verse into living reality as a key foundation of my walk with God. I humbled myself as a creature, in my frailty, mortality and fallibility. I humbled myself in terms of salvation: only Christ could save me when I could not save myself. I humbled myself in terms of my inability to accomplish anything spiritually – apart from Christ I can indeed do absolutely nothing. I humbled myself in terms of my many weaknesses and failings. I humbled myself as a husband, father, son and friend. I humbled myself in terms of my strengths and abilities, recognising that while these could be used by God, when I try to serve him in my own strength I have a terrible habit of failing miserably. It was a painful, yet unforgettable experience of self-abasement, seeking true lowliness of heart before the risen Christ. And then I knew that there was one final step of self-abasement, with regard to the promise that God will lift us up. 'Father,' I prayed, 'I have no right to this promise and so I choose to humble myself before you, discovering my rightful, lowly place with no strings attached, no impatience or presumed insistence upon a swift lifting up.' Whether God raises us up or keeps us low, we must make it a constant priority to humble ourselves and keep walking in humility, both in his presence and in our attitude to others.

One couple who frequently provide hospitality for well-known Christians told me that, while some prominent leaders show graciousness and humility, others have become proud, pushy and intolerant. This should never be. Those who truly humble themselves before God will inevitably and naturally find themselves walking in humility before others. Far from imposing imperious demands, we should be genuinely grateful, even surprised, when we receive any expressions of appreciation, recognition or assistance. The way of the Master is the way of self-giving love and servanthood, never self-aggrandisement, or the pursuit of fame, prestige and power.

Self test

What are the qualities, abilities and achievements that matter most in your life? Could you be in any danger of cultivating a social or religious pedigree?

2

Release from Poor Self-image

The journey into humility is very hard and long for some believers, since new mountain ranges of pride keep soaring to the heights in the hidden terrain of our hearts. For others, all this talk about pride is bewildering and perplexing. Their daily struggle is not to cut themselves down to size but to prevent themselves sinking entirely out of sight in a swamp of self-recrimination.

Every morning was an ordeal for Mary because every mirror said to her that she was too fat, too tall, too ugly. In fact she was of average height, slender and pretty, but her lack of self-esteem came as a distorting lens between herself and the mirror. When her reflection showed an attractive young woman, all Mary could see was her own deficiencies. Her magazines did little to help: the cult of idealised beauty, wasp-waisted and waif-like, creates an unreal image, often less to do with real womanhood than clever make-up, plastic surgery and the tricks of computer-enhanced photography.

Steven's sense of failure came from too many comparisons with his brother. In the eyes of his parents and friends, Steven knew success, both on the playing fields and in exams. But Steven's brother was a renaissance man: if he tried a new sport he was sure to win; if he studied a new subject he was sure to excel. Instead of finding self-worth within himself, Steven tried to develop a sense of his own value by making comparisons with his brother. Unfortunately this meant that Steven set little value on his life, because in competition with his brother the best he could ever hope for was second.

Pamela's poor self-image was rooted in parental rejection. At five her mother announced that she was now too old for cuddles or holding hands. From the moment she was first sent away to school until her graduation from college, not once did she know a moment of affection or approval. Her parents faithfully paid the bills and sent an allowance, but never once did they show her any love. The result was that, inside an extremely successful businesswoman, there was a little girl, vulnerable and insecure, desperately needing to know that someone could really love her.

For those who struggle with poor self-worth, there is a desperate need to discover a secure foundation on which to build and there is none better than the gospel of Jesus Christ. Every single one of us is made in the image of God (Gen. 1:27). We are knit together in our mother's womb, fashioned as unique individuals by God's personal touch (Ps. 139:13–16). God will never forget us, and he calls us each by name (Isa. 43:1, 49:14–16; Heb. 13:5). When Christ died for the world, he died for each of us personally (John 3:16). The Holy Spirit comes to each believer, bringing to us the personal love of God and testifying within us that we have truly become the adopted children of God (Rom. 8:16).

Just as the gospel demands that we lower our selves, when pride has raised us up too high, those sunk in despondency and self-rejection are lifted up with new hope by the same gospel. To those struggling in the quicksand of poor self-worth, God provides the definitive way of escape, establishing a new sense of personal worth, stable and secure, built upon the threefold immovable bedrock of the promises of Scripture, Christ's death for us on the cross and the gift of the Spirit, who pours divine love into our hearts (Rom. 5:5).

A refrain of self-esteem

I am made in God's image,
redeemed by Christ's death,
adopted by the Father
and indwelt by the Spirit.
His Word has declared me a person of great worth.
Who am I to dispute his decree?

3

Word and Spirit, Mind and Heart

God makes himself available to us in every dimension of our being, never restricting his coming to some specialised, religious, Sundays-only compartment of our lives. Paul told the Philippians that he prayed for them to abound more and more in love. His approach is holistic and integrative, for he prays that this supernatural abundance of love will have an impact upon their thinking, enabling them to grow in knowledge and wisdom and the ability to discern what is right (Phil. 1:9–10).

When Paul wrote to the Philippians he was under house arrest. Each morning he was chained to a Roman guard, or possibly two, one on each arm. He had good reason to suppose that his martyrdom was imminent. However, Paul was aware of another kind of guard upon his life, which was more powerful than the Roman soldiers: the peace of God that passes understanding was guarding both his mind and his heart (Phil. 4:7). In encouraging the Philippians to seek this peace, Paul is offering no mere theory. His spirituality had been tested and proven in the crucible of extreme hardship. He emphasises that this peace comes to guard both mind and heart, because we need the guardianship of peace over what we think and at the same time over what we feel, faced with life's pressures. Paul had discovered that he could receive God's peace rising up within him as a guard both upon his thoughts about his captivity and also upon how he felt.

This glorious integration of mind and heart, doctrine and experience, is all too often missing from the Church today. Some churches encourage a healthy and vigorous mind, providing solid teaching and a good, clear grasp of biblical doctrine. But when it comes to heart level encounter with the love of God they back off. The general impression is that it is prudent to avoid spiritual experiences since they are at best superfluous to a sound Christian mind, at worst either dangerous or deluded.

Other churches encourage a healthy and vigorous openness to the Spirit, providing frequent opportunities to grow in living encounter with God. But when it comes to a mind level encounter with the truth of God they back off. The general impression is that it is prudent to avoid using the mind too much, since the organ of the intellect is at best superfluous to spiritual well-being, at worst a source of dryness and doubts.

I spoke with a group of students from one large English city who complained that all the city-centre churches invited them to make a stark choice. Some were strong on biblical preaching and the life of the mind. Others were strong on vibrant worship and an experiential spirituality. The Church has suffered for far too long from this false antithesis. How much longer must we suffer from Christians who are strong-minded with withered hearts, or big-hearted with empty heads!

The Bible provides a third way, rejecting our polarisations and calling us, clearly and consistently, to a creative integration. We are called to be strong-minded and open-hearted: to study the Scriptures *and* to experience the love of God. We can sum up this integration by saying that we want to live as Word and Spirit Christians and to build up churches that are strong in both Word and Spirit. The Spirit is always concerned to help us cherish and understand the Word. He inspired it, he guards it and he brings it alive to our minds (John 14:26, 16:13–15; 2 Tim. 1:14, 3:16–17). At the same time, the Word consistently witnesses to the living reality of the Spirit of God who gave inspiration to its human authors. The Word is never a book of theoretical doctrine alone, but is rather the unique and revelatory Book of truth on fire. We grow in knowledge of God by living as people of the Book, but the Book always points beyond itself, calling us to be people of the Spirit.

The God of self-giving love invites us to keep receiving and not to restrict that receiving to a single, narrow aspect of our life. He created us as complex yet integrated beings. And he comes to us in our complexity, to head and heart, by Word and Spirit, inspiring us to study hard and to think deeply and at the same time inviting and encouraging us to open our hearts and lives to fresh encounters with his awesome presence, his holiness, glory and love.

Personal meditation

Some Christians tend towards Word without Spirit, others to Spirit without Word. The full Christian inheritance invites us to embrace Word and Spirit to the full. Do you have a natural bias to lean to one more than the other? How can we maintain a healthy and dynamic balance between Word and Spirit?

4

Experiencing Love

Throughout the New Testament Christ's death and resurrection are declared emphatically and unequivocally to be the definitive demonstration of the love of God in redemptive action. Whatever our personal circumstances and experiences, nothing can diminish the Christian certainty that 'God was reconciling the world to himself in Christ' (2 Cor. 5:19). Here is the irreducible, immovable core of Christian hope. Whatever my circumstances, my feelings, my prospects, of these three things I am always certain: Christ has died, Christ is risen and Christ will come again.

For the Ephesians, Paul prayed that with their minds they would grasp as best they could the transcendent enormity of the dimensions of divine love, supremely made manifest to humankind through the cross of Christ. Once again Paul's approach is holistic, for he immediately prays for a profound experiential encounter with this love.

> *And I pray that you, being rooted and established in love, may have power, together with all the saints, to grasp how wide and long and high and deep is the love of Christ, and to know this love that surpasses knowledge – that you may be filled to the measure of all the fulness of God.*

Ephesians 3:17–19

Paul's concern is that believers will use their minds to the full in exploring and reflecting upon heavenly love, but then that they will enter into this love beyond the limited capacity of their brainpower. Paul's great hope, therefore, is not only that the Ephesians will be thinking Christians, loving God as best they may with their minds, but also that they will be open-hearted Christians, not restricting their experience of God's love within the confines of their little grey cells.

The unchanging fact of God's love for us in Christ needs to be absorbed into our lives so that it is not merely a statement to which we give assent but a living, dynamic truth, shaping and governing our daily living. This is how the New Testament writers understand Christian doctrine, not as something exclusively for the intellectually curious or the argumentative, but a framework of revealed truth that gives us a reliable, healthy, Christ-centred perspective upon the whole of life. Experiences of God's love may come and go, but the truth of God's love for us is irreversible, determined irrevocably from all eternity and demonstrated conclusively at the cross of Christ.

The extent to which God loves us is repeatedly explored in the New Testament. He loved us when we were far off, even when we were his enemies (Rom. 5:6, 8, 10). He loves us extravagantly and eternally (Eph. 1:4, 8). He takes the initiative of saving grace and loves us lavishly before we begin to love him (1 John 3:1, 4:10, 19). He loves us as his adoptive children (Rom. 8:16). The most extreme definition of the extent of God's love is found on Jesus' lips. If Jesus had not made such a claim, it is doubtful that any of his followers would have ever dared to make such a suggestion. When praying his high-priestly prayer, shortly before his arrest and execution, Jesus makes his most astonishing declaration: God the Father loves each one of us just as he loves Jesus (John 17:23). The measure of love with which the Father is devoted eternally to his own dear Son is the measure with which he loves us. He not only loves us enough to rescue us, but in the extravagance of his grace he loves us to the uttermost.

Some Christians find it easier to remember to have another cup of coffee than to continue to live in the light of God's love in Christ. For such I commend the simple practice of the coffee prayer. When we have another cup of coffee at regular intervals through the day, on automatic caffeine pilot, we can turn this habit to our spiritual advantage with this simple resolve. For an entire week, every time you have a new cup of coffee steaming before you, pause for a moment and pray: 'Father, I thank you so much that you love me as much as you love Jesus, and that is why he died in my place.'

When people learn a foreign language they develop an active vocabulary of the words they are able to use, and a passive vocabulary, which they can understand but never use. In the same way, Christians usually operate with active and passive doctrines: the passive doctrines are the ones to which we give theoretical assent but which fail to influence the way we see life or feel about ourselves. The regular repetition of even such a simple prayer can help to shift the doctrine of God's love from passive to active, from 'God loves humanity' to 'It's so wonderful that God really does love me!'

The first Christians not only took delight in celebrating the glorious truth of God's love for us in Christ, they also taught the possibility and privilege of encountering this love in personal experience.

> *And hope does not disappoint us, for God has poured out his love into our hearts by the Holy Spirit, whom he has given us.*
>
> Romans 5:5

This is far more than a detached declaration of truth. Nor is Paul suggesting that a fortunate few have an occasional and rarefied mystical encounter with the Spirit of Christ. Although he had not yet met the Christians at Rome, Paul clearly did not think that he was introducing a novel concept or describing something completely unknown to the Roman church. On the contrary, Paul is confident that this would be a familiar, even universal experience: the love of God can be shed abroad in the heart of every single Christian believer.

At the time of the Great Awakening, the opportunity for an inward encounter with the love of God was frequently emphasised. In his own conversion, John Wesley spoke about his heart being 'strangely warmed'. A number of preachers in the revival spoke about the need to encounter the 'felt Christ'. Both Whitefield and Edwards describe individuals crying out in meetings, 'He has come! He has come!' In an age of nominal assent to the Christian faith, when many churchgoers knew nothing about the need for personal, saving faith, this emphasis upon the felt Christ was distinctive and crucial.

As we recover a biblical emphasis upon experiencing the Holy Spirit and receiving God's love inwardly, we must be careful to avoid the equal and opposite dangers connected with cynicism and gullibility. First, some suffer from an instinctive suspicion that if someone has a spiritual experience it is far more likely to be demonic than divine: this instinctive negativity is deeply corrosive of authentic biblical spirituality. At the opposite extreme, there are those who attempt to universalise the secondary details of their particular spiritual experience: if their heart was warmed, everyone's heart must be warmed; if they trembled outwardly, everyone must tremble. What the New Testament emphasises is the availability of divine love: the symptoms, side effects and intensity of our encounter are likely to vary enormously from person to person, and from temperament to temperament. We need to reject the dismissive narrowness of cynical suspicion, and at the same time reject the opposite narrowness of compulsory conformity in secondary issues. What matters is that with mind and heart, in understanding and spiritual encounter, we grow in a knowledge of the love of God that has the power to touch every dimension of human existence, sharpening our intellect, enriching our relationships and strangely warming our hearts.

Personal reflection

Can you identify any key moments when you have experienced a deep encounter with the love of God? If so, what difference has that made in your life?

5

Walking through Darkness

Just as there is nothing more wonderful than a personal encounter with the love of God, poured in great abundance into our inmost being by the Holy Spirit, there is nothing more perplexing than to experience the absence of God.

For some, a spiritual desert may be entered as a result of bereavement. The way we cope and adjust to loss often includes an emotional withdrawal that may affect us spiritually as well as in other relationships and aspects of life. Despite the fact that many people today seem to expect a full 'recovery' within days of a loved one's funeral, bereavement is a slow, continuing and sometimes arduous process. There is a predictable emotional cycle, through which most people pass. First there is *shock* at the news, then *numbness*, an emotional detachment as if living in a bell jar, cut off from normal life and even the pain of the loss. A release of *grief* is likely to follow, which can be followed by *anger* as we look for someone to blame – often ourselves, a doctor, or even God. *Denial* arises as we look for comfort in the thought that perhaps it has all been a terrible dream and our loved one is still alive. This can happen almost immediately, or it can overtake us in the coming months, for example when someone suddenly finds themselves laying a place at the meal table for the person who has died. Finally the reality of the death is *embraced*. That certainly does not mean that we have 'got over it', but it does confirm that we have begun to learn how to live with the continuing sense of loss.

This cycle of emotional responses is almost invariably passed through several times. If the bereavement process is moving forward in a healthy way, it may feel something like ascending a spiral staircase: we circle through the same emotional sequence, but gradually we gain height, leaving behind the depths of the initial experience of loss. Where the process gets stuck, our bereavement becomes incomplete and we continue to be traumatised by our loss. I think of Catherine, who was only seven when her father died. In an attempt to protect the child, her mother and grandparents were always telling her not to cry. As a result, in adulthood she continued to be trapped within an unresolved experience of bereavement: she had never been able to give expression to the grief that was locked up within, an agonising sense of loss and even rejection. At the same time, childhood denial of the painful reality had stayed with her, so that she continued to nurse an irrational hope: 'Daddy hasn't really died and one day he will come and be with me again.'

False hope and repressed grief sat heavily upon Catherine's life. Her capacity to give and receive love was constantly undermined by a deadening inner void. There was an emptiness in her relationships with those close to her and an emptiness in her relationship with God. Only through the sustained support of sensitive counselling and prayer for healing could Catherine experience release. It was a great joy to all who had sought to provide support through her overshadowed days when Catherine finally broke through to a new sense of release and wholeness, liberated from the prison-house of a blocked bereavement and able once more to give and receive love. At last she was able to be immersed in the love of God, and soon she was able to enter into a happy and secure marriage.

A profound sense of disappointment is another emotionally intense experience that can have a cavernous spiritual impact. While some discover a new closeness to God in a time of need, others can feel more cut off, more spiritually disengaged, than at any previous moment in their lives. Richard had set his eyes upon a particular promotion. He knew that others were encouraging his appointment, and he sensed God's call to the task. Over the previous two years he had turned down two other strategic jobs, not wanting to let down new colleagues by moving on again prematurely.

When Richard was turned down for the promotion he had anticipated, it was as if he fell into a black hole. Although he knew in principle that God had not deserted him, his career path had suddenly become confusing. He lost his sense of direction and purpose, and began to fear that he might have misheard God altogether. If he was not the right man for the job he had been working towards, perhaps he had made a disastrous mistake in turning down the other opportunities. Richard told me that his problem was not losing faith in God, but rather losing faith in himself. For the next few months he lived in that black hole of uncertainty and self-doubt, wondering whether he had parked himself in a permanent lay-by, a man whose potential was now destined never to be fulfilled, whose life might become more about marking time than making a difference for Jesus Christ.

Richard's friends did their best to reassure him, suggesting that new, unexpected and even better opportunities were sure eventually to arise. He accepted their positive perspective in principle, and had no desire to wallow in self-pity. At an emotional level it seemed he had to embrace the shadows of disappointment before new hope could be born. For several weeks, in worship and prayer, the only picture that repeatedly came to his mind was of a rose bush, pruned hard to the ground, in a bleak and desolate landscape. There was no way of rushing his inner reappraisal and recovery. Richard had to learn how to walk patiently in the truth of his faith as he awaited the eventual new dawn.

Whether through bereavement or profound disappointment, depression or some other life crisis, we can experience a season of spiritual barrenness. There is nothing more crushing than someone suggesting that such a season of life is unnecessary or self-inflicted. The absence of any experience of God is a perplexing mystery and yet a spiritual reality through which some are required to walk. They need our patience, love and kind support, not a sweeping, insensitive or judgmental reaction.

At such a time, when the Holy Spirit's presence seems to have been withdrawn from our lives, we need to lean more heavily upon the Lord's Supper and the Bible. Whether or not we feel God's love, we can still break bread, drink wine, and seek to feed on Christ by faith in our hearts. The great meal of the Church, established by Jesus Christ, is an experienced sign of the love of God, and a continuing source of comfort, hope and strength.

At the same time, the promises of Scripture speak to us in adversity and when we plumb emotional and spiritual depths. Isaiah's prophetic comfort to those suffering the powerlessness and despondency of the Babylonian exile and Paul's resounding words to the Romans both issue a clarion call of comfort, promising God's love and protection even when our spiritual experience of that love seems to be nothing other than a deadening void.

> *But now this is what the LORD says –*
> *he who created you, O Jacob,*
> *he who formed you, O Israel:*
> *'Fear not, for I have redeemed you;*

> *I have summoned you by name; you are mine.*
> *When you pass through the waters,*
> *I will be with you;*
> *and when you pass through the rivers,*
> *they will not sweep over you.*
> *When you walk through the fire,*
> *you will not be burned;*
> *the flames will not set you ablaze ...*
> *Since you are precious and honoured in my sight,*
> *and because I love you ...*
>
> Isaiah 43:1–4

> *Who shall separate us from the love of Christ? Shall trouble or*
> *hardship or persecution or famine or nakedness or danger or sword?*
> *... No, in all these things we are more than conquerors through*
> *him who loved us. For I am convinced that neither death nor life,*
> *neither angels nor demons, neither the present nor the future, nor*
> *any powers, neither height nor depth, nor anything else in all*
> *creation, will be able to separate us from the love of God that is*
> *in Christ Jesus our Lord.*
>
> Romans 8:35–9

As ever, Paul is not providing an empty promise, a mere rhetorical flourish, for at the time of writing he had already known personally all the adversities that he lists except the last – the sword – and even that awaited him in his eventual execution by beheading.

The Scriptures never promise us an easy life, exempt from fire or famine, danger or martyrdom. What we are guaranteed, even in the most tormented or dismal of personal circumstances, is God's protection and the promise that we are eternally inseparable from the love of God in Christ.

In difficult and extremely demanding circumstances we can

feel as if our grip upon God is very weak, clinging by our fingertips to the rock-face of truth. But the great promises of Scripture offer a very different perspective: coping with life, but never alone. Babies are born with an instinctive reflex to fasten upon anything that comes into their hand. All their fingers close tight, but the entire clasp of such a tiny hand can grip no more than a single adult finger. If the adult then closes their hand in turn, they grasp far more than the baby's fingers and hand, for the whole of the baby's arm comes within their clasp. Even so, if our grip upon God seems slight and tenuous, and our experience of God seems a deadening void, the promises of Scripture remain sure: no matter how weak our hold on God, we remain clasped and secure in the mighty hand of Christ. We remain safe in his grip.

Personal reflection

Look back to a season of darkness, whether in your own life or the life of someone close to you. How did the Word and Spirit keep you going?

6

Receiving Prayer

One of the greatest privileges of belonging to the Church is being prayed for by other Christians. In Chapter 4 we explored some principles and guidelines for a local church prayer ministry team; now we turn to consider what it means to be on the receiving end of personal prayer ministry. When Paul was converted, the risen Christ dealt with him upon the road without human assistance. Christ revealed himself and Paul repented and came to faith, getting up from the ground blind in his eyes but with his spiritual sight illumined at last (Acts 9:3–9). Having done so much by direct intervention, it seems extraordinary that Christ sent Paul into the city with three crucial matters unresolved. Only when Ananias came to pray with him did Paul experience healing for his eyes, being filled with the Holy Spirit, and receiving a prophetic word about his future ministry among the Gentiles (Acts 9:10–19).

Clearly the risen Christ had no need to work via Ananias, so why did he adopt this method? Surely it was to establish as soon as possible in Paul's life the Christian principle of interdependence. Paul was so intellectually brilliant, his Damascus road encounter with the risen Christ so direct and unforgettable, he could easily have launched out on a trajectory of heroic isolation, with the proud illusion that he had no need of the ministry of others. How much better, immediately after his wonderful conversion, that he should discover the extraordinary privilege of receiving prayer ministry at the hands of an ordinary believer from the church in Damascus.

All too often this kind of praying has been marginalised. In some churches it is perfectly permissible to be prayed with, but such ministry tends to be reserved for unusual, even exceptional circumstances. The unspoken implications are obvious: if all else has been tried and has failed, and if you are really desperate, the last resort of all is to ask for prayer ministry. However, it seems to me that being on the receiving end of prayer ministry is not a sign of weakness, but a sign of wisdom. We are all fallible and frail, and we can all be strengthened by the encouragement and faith of our brothers and sisters.

In other churches the ministry is more widely and regularly available, but there is one category of Christian never seen to receive prayer, namely the leaders. It seems as if ordinary Christians can benefit from prayer ministry, while leaders are exempt from such needs so that their only task is to make this ministry available for others. The implications are obvious: prayer ministry is available, but not for leaders, and so, if you are a leader or aspire to become a leader, the one thing to avoid at all costs is to be seen receiving prayer! Leaders are needed who are prepared to model an authentic spirituality, which includes demonstrating our own vulnerability, fallibility and profound continuing need for the inspiration of the Spirit of Christ, rather than perpetuating the sad, stale myths of omnicompetence and spiritual self-sufficiency. When there are opportunities for prayer ministry, leaders need to be encouraged to be seen taking their turn to be on the receiving end.

In order to benefit from prayer ministry, we need to cultivate an attitude of openness and receptivity. Imagine someone preparing to receive communion who was so busy talking that they never paused long enough for bread and wine to pass their lips.

Or imagine someone who took a portion of bread but then simply gazed upon it as a detached observer, failing to take the opportunity to eat it and 'feed on Christ by faith in your heart, with thanksgiving'. Just as we come to communion to eat and drink, and not simply to talk or observe, we need to come for prayer ministry with a willingness to receive from the Holy Spirit. This means that we need to take time out from talking: the person who is constantly praying aloud while receiving prayer shows little or no desire to listen to God or receive anew from the Spirit. We also need to take our defences down: if we do not have confidence in those praying, this will not be possible. Of course, there are moments of fear and anxiety faced with even a small measure of the power and the glory of the living God, but there is no one better to bring our fears before than Jesus Christ. He understands our fears and will gently relieve us of them when we are prepared to hand them over. There is only one way to be ready for a new and living surrender to Christ's Lordship and love, and that is to choose to be open to God, no strings attached.

For me personally, there is huge benefit in encouraging others to pray for me, not only for the needs and opportunities of the coming days, but that I may know spiritual replenishment and refreshment. Sometimes there is a moment of revelatory encounter, through a Scripture, a prophetic word or the direct impress of the Holy Spirit. On other occasions, it is simply good to set time aside before the risen Christ, enjoying something of the infinitude of his love and surrendering afresh to his Lordship.

In many churches, communion is an ideal time to begin exploring prayer ministry. Especially in churches where people are already moving to the front to receive the bread and wine, it is a fairly small and safe innovation to stay for prayer or to step to one side where members of the prayer team are available. When I preached recently at a Pentecost celebration in an

Anglican cathedral, I was delighted to see the Bishop place himself in line to receive prayer as soon as the distribution of communion was complete. His example gave encouragement to the cautious and permission to those who needed reassurance that receiving personal prayer, other than when being confirmed, was a legitimate practice in a cathedral service.

In my own experience, it has been extraordinarily enriching to receive prayer ministry and an incalculable privilege to pray for others in this way. Prayer ministry is a delight both to give and to receive, a wonderful expression of the love of God in action. It is a ministry that I would like to encourage, with appropriate pastoral sensitivity, wisdom and oversight, in every local church.

We have sought to explore in this little book some of the key principles and practices of walking with God. We have examined growing in relationship with God as Father, learning to be still in the divine presence, responding to God's holiness and our sinfulness, praying for others, finding space for solitary prayer, meditating upon the Scriptures and the cross, and learning to receive more of God's loving, holy and empowering presence. The journey into prayer can always take us further, with more to discover of our need for God and the immensity of his patience and love, glory and grace. My prayer, as you come to the end of these pages, is that your walk with God will be ever more rich and deep, freed from the ruts of shallowness and predictability, and kept fresh in the glorious interaction of the Word and the Spirit. Keep going, seeking to walk ever closer with God.

Personal goal setting

What three practical steps would help you in the coming year to explore and pursue a closer walk with God? It may help to write them down and see what progress you have made in three, six, nine and twelve months.

7

Bible Meditation

ROMANS 12:1–2

*Therefore, I urge you, brothers and sisters, in view of God's mercy,
to offer your bodies as living sacrifices, holy and pleasing to God
– this is your spiritual act of worship. Do not conform any longer
to the pattern of this world, but be transformed by the renewing of
your mind. Then you will be able to test and approve what God's
will is – his good, pleasing and perfect will.*

Motivation for the sacrifice

Paul provides two good reasons to offer ourselves as living
sacrifices. First, it is a response to the self-sacrifice of God:
in the light of the cross we give ourselves back to the God
who gave himself for us. Second, when believers surrender
themselves in this way, God takes pleasure in our sacrifice.

The nature of the sacrifice

Paul emphasises that as we surrender to God the sacrifice includes
our body. This reminds us that the gospel is profoundly holistic,
for we can learn to walk with God in every dimension of our

existence, not only at church, but at home, at work and at leisure. What's more, we offer ourselves as *living* sacrifices. Someone once said that the trouble with living sacrifices is that they keep crawling back off the altar. As a living sacrifice, it is not enough to present ourselves to God once. We have to keep coming back in fresh surrender.

Resistance to the sacrifice

The pattern of this world is always drawing and beguiling us towards conformity. We see this with the power of peer pressure among teenagers. It is also obvious in the power of advertising and the media. Our world is filled with a constant seduction towards conformity in a self-centred materialism that has no time for God, the Ten Commandments and the self-giving love of the Cross. Paul urges us no longer to conform to the standard worldly patterns of thought and behaviour.

The result of the sacrifice

Out of surrender come wisdom and peace: the wisdom of growing in an understanding of God's perfect will, and the peace of choosing to walk in the ways of Christ, seeing life from a heavenly perspective.

Even now, you may want to respond to the scriptural invitation and offer yourself anew in willing surrender to the risen Christ. A new day, a new self-sacrifice to the God of self-giving love.

Poems, Prayers and Hymns for Reflection

DENIAL

(Through the broken rhyme pattern that is eventually restored in the last line, Herbert expresses the desolation of spiritual barrenness and yet his resolute hope for a new dawn.)

When my devotions could not pierce
Thy silent ears;
Then was my heart broken, as was my verse:
My breast was full of fears,
And disorder:

My bent thoughts, like a brittle bow,
Did fly asunder:
Each took his way; some would to pleasures go,
Some to the wars and thunder
Of alarms.

As good go anywhere, they say,
As to benumb
Both knees and heart, in crying night and day,
Come, come, my God, O come,
But no hearing.

O that thou shouldst give dust a tongue
To cry to thee,
And then not hear it crying! All day long
My heart was in my knee,
But no hearing.

Therefore my soul lay out of sight,
Untun'd, unstrung:
My feeble spirit, unable to look right,
Like a nipped blossom, hung
Discontented.

O cheer and tune my heartless breast,
Defer no time;
That so thy favours granting my request,
They and my mind may chime,
And mend my rhyme.

George Herbert, 1593–1633

LOVE
(A sonnet about the great and climactic coming communion in
heaven – Luke 12:37)

Love bade me welcome: yet my soul drew back,
Guilty of dust and sin.
But quick-eyed Love, observing me grow slack
From my first entrance in,
Drew nearer to me, sweetly questioning,
If I lacked anything.

A guest, I answered, worthy to be here:
Love said, You shall be he.
I the unkind, ungrateful? Ah my dear,
I cannot look on thee.
Love took my hand, and smiling did reply,
Who made the eyes but I?

Truth, Lord, but I have marred them: let my shame
Go where it doth deserve.
And know you not, says Love, who bore the blame?
My dear, then I will serve.
You must sit down, says Love, and taste my meat:
So I did sit and eat.

George Herbert, 1593–1633

HOLY SONNET XIV

Batter my heart, three personed God; for, you
As yet but knock, breathe, shine, and seek to mend;
That I may rise, and stand, o'erthrow me, and bend
Your force, to break, blow, burn and make me new.
I, like an usurped town, to another due,
Labour to admit you, but O, to no end,
Reason, your viceroy in me, me should defend,
But is captived, and proves weak or untrue.
Yet dearly I love you, and would be loved fain,
But am betrothed unto your enemy:
Divorce me, untie, or break that knot again,
Take me to you, imprison me, for I
Except you enthral me, never shall be free,
Nor ever chaste, except you ravish me.

John Donne, 1573–1631

Come down, O Love Divine,
Seek thou this soul of mine,
And visit it with thine own ardour glowing;
O Comforter, draw near,
Within my heart appear,
And kindle it, thy holy flame bestowing.

O let it freely burn,
Till earthly passions turn
To dust and ashes, in its heat consuming;
And let thy glorious light,
Shine ever on my sight,
And clothe me round, the while my path illuming.

Let holy charity
Mine outward vesture be,
And lowliness become mine inner clothing;
True lowliness of heart,
Which takes the humbler part,
And o'er its own shortcomings weeps with loathing.

And so the yearning strong
With which the soul will long,
Shall far outpass the power of human telling;
For none can guess its grace,
Till he become the place
Wherein the Holy Spirit makes his dwelling.

Bianco da Siena d. 1434
Translated by Richard Littledale, 1833–90

O God the Holy Ghost who art Light unto thine elect,
Evermore enlighten us.
Thou who art Fire of Love,
Evermore enkindle us.
Thou who are Lord and Giver of Life,
Evermore live in us.
Thou who bestowest sevenfold grace,
Evermore replenish us.
As the wind is thy symbol,
So forward our goings.
As the dove,
So launch us heavenwards.
As water,
So purify our spirits.
As a cloud,
So abate our temptations.
As dew,
So revive our languor.
As fire,
So purge our dross.

Christina Rossetti, 1830–94

God be in my head
And in my understanding.
God be in mine eyes
And in my looking.
God be in my mouth
And in my speaking.

God be in my heart
And in my thinking.
God be at mine end
And at my departing.
                    Sarum Primer

A hymn by Charles Wesley

O thou who camest from above,
The pure, celestial fire t'impart,
Kindle a flame of sacred love
On the mean altar of my heart;
There let it for thy glory burn
With inextinguishable blaze,
And trembling to its source return,
In humble prayer, and fervent praise.

Jesus, confirm my heart's desire
To work, and speak, and think for thee;
Still let me guard the holy fire,
And still stir up thy gift in me:
Ready for all thy perfect will
My acts of faith and love repeat,
Till death thy endless mercies seal,
And make my sacrifice complete.

Further Reading

Augustine	*Confessions*
Benedict	*The Rule of St Benedict*
Bernard of Clairvaux	*On the Love of God*
David Brainerd (ed. J. Edwards)	*The Life and Death of David Brainerd*
John Bunyan	*Pilgrim's Progress*
	Grace Abounding
Alan Ecclestone	*Yes to God*
Jonathan Edwards	*The Religious Affections*
Sarah Edwards	*Journal* (found within the memoir of Jonathan Edwards, *Complete Works*, vol. I)
Ruth Etchells (ed.)	*Praying with the English Poets*
Richard Foster	*Celebration of Discipline*
	Prayer
Marjory Foyle	*Honourably Wounded*
Francis of Assisi	*The Little Flowers of St Francis*
James Gordon	*Evangelical Spirituality*
O. Hallesby	*Prayer*
David Hanes (ed.)	*My Path of Prayer*
Walter Hilton	*The Stairway of Perfection*
James Houston	*The Transforming Friendship*
Joyce Huggett	*Listening to God*
	The Smile of Love
Basil Hume	*Searching for God*
John of the Cross	*The Dark Night of the Soul*
Julian of Norwich	*Revelations of Divine Love*
Thomas Kelly	*A Testament of Devotion*
Thomas à Kempis	*The Imitation of Christ*

William Law	*A Serious Call to a Devout and Holy Life*
Brother Lawrence	*The Practice of the Presence of God*
Ignatius Loyola	*The Spiritual Exercises*
Gordon Macdonald	*Ordering Your Private World*
	Restoring Your Spiritual Passion
Floyd McLung	*The Father Heart of God*
Nether Springs Community	*A Northumbrian Office*
John Newton	*Letters*
Henry Nouwen	*The Genessee Diary*
	Creative Ministry
	The Wounded Healer
J. I. Packer	*Knowing God*
Blaise Pascal	*Pensées*
Eugene Peterson	*A Long Obedience in the Same Direction*
Richard Rolle	*The Fire of Love*
J. C. Ryle	*Holiness*
Francis de Sales	*Introduction to the Devout Life*
Ray Simpson	*Exploring Celtic Spirituality*
Jeremy Taylor	*Holy Living*
Abbé de Tourville	*Letters of Spiritual Direction*
Simon Tugwell	*Ways of Imperfection*
Evelyn Underhill	*The Spiritual Life*
Charles Wesley	*Hymns* (one excellent selected edition is *A Flame of Love*, ed. T. Dudley-Smith)
John Wesley	*Journals*
George Whitefield	*Journals*

ANONYMOUS WRITINGS AND COMPILATIONS

Cloud of Unknowing
The Lives and Sayings of the Desert Fathers
The Philokalia
Rule for a New Brother
Theologica Germanica